UNLOCKED

Embrace Your
Greatness

———

Find the Flow

———

Discover
Success

GEORGE
MUMFORD

HarperOne
An Imprint of HarperCollins*Publishers*

Excerpts on pages 193 and 204 from Thich Nhat Hanh,
Call Me by My True Names, Parallax Press, 1999, 2002.
Reprinted with permission.

HarperCollins books may be purchased for educational, business,
or sales promotional use. For information, please email the Special
Markets Department at SPsales@harpercollins.com.

FIRST EDITION

Library of Congress Cataloging-in-Publication Data has been
applied for.

ISBN 978-0-06-321009-7
ISBN 978-0-06-333784-8 (Int'l)

23 24 25 26 27 LBC 5 4 3 2 1

This, I believe, is the great Western truth: that each of us is a completely unique creature and that, if we are ever to give any gift to the world, it will have to come out of our own experience and fulfillment of our own potentialities, not someone else's.

—Joseph Campbell

CONTENTS

BEING TRUE TO YOURSELF

———

Our divine potential [is] most effective when it starts to become automatic, when it becomes unconscious or subconscious. When this happens, people do exactly what they know to do—not what they think they know, not what they should know, not what other people say they know. . . . As the Chinese say: to know and not to do is, in fact, not to know.

—Maya Angelou

How can we move from bracing for failure to waiting for fulfillment? Is there any other question as significant for our performance or our happiness?

I've been around greatness all my life. I roomed with basketball great Dr. J (Julius Erving) in college, and I've worked with the elite of elite athletes, including Michael Jordan, Scottie Pippen, Kobe Bryant, and Shaquille O'Neal. There is no doubt these athletes were tremendously gifted, loaded with talent. But what I've learned from my association with them is that natural ability wasn't what made them great. What made them so exceptional was that they were what I call *unlocked*—they were in close touch with that part of themselves that was most truly who they were. *That* is what allowed them to develop their potential in the way they did.

Greatness can be discovered in each and every one of us. It's not just the Kobes of the world; I've seen that greatness emerge in men convicted of murder serving consecutive life sentences in prison. This potential is not a euphemistic, feel-good fantasy. It is real and tangible and attainable for all.

I know this from working with everyone from elite athletes and powerful CEOs to those pushed to the margins of society. I also know this from the arc of my own life. I'm almost forty years into recovery from alcoholism and heroin addiction. My life changed through prayer and meditation and through service. I dedicated myself to working with people from Yale to jail, from locker rooms to boardrooms. I know that in order to keep what I have learned, I have to give it away. In order to keep learning and growing and expanding, I have to teach. That's what I'm doing in these pages.

My mission has been to help anyone in any place at any time unlock the greatness within them. The greatness within is why we are alive. It is what we have to offer to the world.

A NUMBER OF YEARS AGO, I WAS HIRED BY AN ELITE PREP school to work with their basketball team, particularly their star player, who, the school felt, wasn't living up to his potential.

I drove through the suburbs west of Boston on a cool spring day, passing through an open wrought-iron gate set between stone pillars, and traveled down a long, curving drive lined with lilacs that were just coming into bloom. A student in a navy-blue blazer and fashionably untucked white dress shirt led me out past the groomed soccer fields and rows of empty tennis courts to the athletic complex.

The basketball team, half in home jerseys and half in away, was scrimmaging in one of the gyms. I watched them play for a while. They looked like an undistinguished, well-meaning bunch except for one kid. I knew he was the one that they had hired me to counsel and coach, an African American kid I'll call Khaleel. I had been briefed on him when I took the job. He had been brought to the school on a full scholarship. At six foot five and still growing, he was a skinny-as-a-rail sixteen-year-old, but you could see the NBA body waiting to emerge from his rickety frame. I watched from the sideline as Khaleel drove hard to the hoop, slamming down dunks. He pulled up at the three-point line and drained his outside shot. His long arms and quick hands made him a monster on defense. He got deflections and steals and leaped high to block shots.

Although the team was doing well, due almost entirely to Khaleel's stellar play, the kid had, according to the school psychologist, problems concentrating on his schoolwork; and the psychologist thought that his shoddy grades had been affecting his play during recent games. The team had begun to slip in their league's standings. Khaleel was one of the few Black kids at a predominantly white school, and he had a tremendous amount of pressure on him to perform, justify his full athletic scholarship, and bring home a championship trophy to the school. The psychologist had heard about me from a colleague, and he knew one of Khaleel's heroes was Kobe Bryant.

"I want to be like Kobe," Khaleel told me after we had been introduced during a break in the practice. I had to laugh. I can't tell you how many times I've heard that. Khaleel said he had studied the Kobe Bryant formula for success: focus, practice hard, commit to winning.

I knew from the school psychologist that, like me, Khaleel had come from the hood. Under his cocky swagger, I felt wariness. The tender, genuine parts of him had been encrusted within an affected cool by his tough childhood.

"Teach me Kobe stuff," he said. "I need that mamba mentality."

"Are you willing to do what Kobe was willing to do in order to be the best of the best?" I asked.

"Most *definitely*."

It's one thing to say it, I thought, and it's entirely another thing to do it.

Kobe had adopted the mamba persona, named after the black snake indigenous to Africa, known for its lethal quickness and deadly venom.

Khaleel wanted to become a mamba like his hero; but that, unfortunately, is not the way it works. It's okay to model yourself after those you admire. But in sports or any other pursuit, that's only the beginning. You need something more: you need to find your "gift to the world."

A DEEPER INTELLIGENCE

With his mamba mentality, Kobe was a trailblazer in this regard. When I worked with him, I was living outside Boston in Newton, and I would fly out to LA to work with the Lakers, meeting with players and coaches at the team's sprawling, state-of-the-art practice facility in El Segundo and staying in a nearby hotel.

Kobe and I had an immediate connection. I had roomed with Dr. J—Julius Erving—and played pickup ball with him in college at the University of Massachusetts, Amherst. Kobe's father, Joe Bryant, and Dr. J had been teammates on the Philadelphia 76ers in the 1970s. Kobe immediately saw me as a kind of uncle figure, a seasoned mentor who was as driven and determined as he was and who had a direct connection to his father's generation of Black basketball players. The NBA is now over 75 percent African American, but at that time it was mostly white; in fact, just a decade earlier, in the 1960s, there had been an effort to limit Black players. Kobe, of course, as a student of the game, knew this, and he also knew it on a personal level. His father's move to play in Europe had been in part determined by the way the NBA treated African American players, and that made my connection to the generation of Black players to which his father had belonged all the more significant.

Kobe was a sponge—he took it all in. His curiosity was boundless about anything that could potentially help his game. There are stories of him reaching out to top athletes, cold-calling them at all hours. Same with renowned writers, CEOs, movie stars, famous musicians, and film directors; Kobe was always trying to understand what made them great at what they did and learn from their experience.

I worked with the team, not only using my skills as a meditation teacher but also employing what I'd learned as a therapist and stress reduction expert. I added elements of my training in personal and organizational development and group dynamics. I also did a lot of mental discipline training, which is about directing and sustaining attention, being in the moment, and remaining calm and present regardless of circumstances. I teach this by working with people to create space between any given stimulus we may receive and our response to it. Through mindful breathing—closely following the breath going in and out of the body while carefully tracking our bodily sensations and the pattern of our thoughts—we can all become aware of and extend the space between stimulus and response. If we can extend that space so that we're not automatically and immediately reactive, we will be better able to make wise choices about how to respond to anything coming at us, whether someone is trying to block our jump shot or take advantage of us in a business deal.

When we're responding in a nonreactive way, our choices are not always or even often the result of what we would call decision-making on a conscious level. Especially in sports—and sports at the highest level—the rhythm and pace of the kind of decision-making I'm talking about is breathtaking. It happens beyond conscious thought. A deeper intelligence is at work, and the results can be astounding.

Basketball legend and former Boston Celtics All-Star Bill Russell writes about the apex of this experience in his book *Second Wind: The Memoirs of an Opinionated Man*:

> I could feel my play rise to a new level. . . . It would surround not only me and the other team, [but] even the referees. . . . At that special level, all sorts of odd things happened. The game would be in the white heat of competition, and yet somehow, I wouldn't feel competitive, which is a miracle in itself. I'd be putting out maximum effort, straining, coughing up parts of my lungs as we ran, and yet I never felt the pain. The game would move so quickly that every fake, cut, and pass would be surprising, and yet nothing could surprise me. It was almost as if we were playing in slow motion. During those spells, I could almost sense how the next play would develop and where the next shot would be taken. . . . My premonitions would be consistently correct, and I always felt that I not only knew all the Celtics by heart, but also all the opposing players, and that they knew me. There have been many times in my career when I felt moved or joyful, but these were moments when I had chills pulsing up and down my spine. . . . On the five or ten occasions when the game ended at

that special level, I literally did not care who had won. If we lost,
I'd still be as free and high as a sky hawk.

Russell is writing about being fully unlocked. He describes this
state as a feeling of connection that on rare occasions envelops all
the players and refs; they are inhabited by a kind of group mind,
similar to the intelligence of a flock of birds flying full speed, all
turning together in perfect synchrony. It's what physicist David
Bohn calls the "implicit order" suddenly made manifest and
explicit. It is a feeling of prescience, knowing what's going to
happen before it happens. It's significant that Russell says this
shared unlocked experience happened perhaps only five or ten
times during his career, at the end of games. It is not a state we
generally attain, although researchers today are working to better
understand it and what produces it. Russell is talking about an
extreme instance of what we all sometimes experience as "flow
state" or "optimal experience," terms coined by psychologist
Mihaly Csikszentmihalyi. We could also think of it as being "in
the zone" or being "locked in."

The accomplished people that I've worked with, whether
top-notch athletes or corporate CEOs, or those who have
overcome great hurdles, seem to have the ability to access this
state, perhaps not readily but in a way that allows them to
perform at a consistently high level. My role and work is to
help individuals access this state. Not everyone is ready for it.
There has to be the willingness to go beyond what we feel is
possible, what we think are our limits. This is part of becoming
unlocked.

ALLOWING LIFE TO SPEAK FOR ITSELF

My immediate impression of Kobe was that he was the closest thing to Michael Jordan that I had seen. Same incredible concentration and focus. Same killer instinct. But as we worked together, I began to see that Kobe really was his own thing. He had found what he wanted to gift to the world, and he was incomparable.

This was driven home when he was injured in a game against the San Antonio Spurs. He dislocated the little finger of his right hand—his shooting hand. Gary Vitti, head trainer for the Lakers, walked Kobe over to the Lakers' bench. They stopped and Kobe bent over slightly; Vitti was close to him, talking to him, taking his hand; and then Kobe gasped and heaved, absorbing the pain as Vitti popped the finger back into place. Kobe held the hand up in front his face with a look of curiosity and assessment and wiggled his fingers. Then he looked over at San Antonio's perennial superstar Tim Duncan and made a joke. Duncan laughed. Kobe, being Kobe, then went right on playing. Which was remarkable, given that the injury turned out to be much more than a simple dislocation. After fuller examination, it turned out that Kobe had a torn ligament and a bone fracture in that finger. Typically, both injuries would keep an NBA player out of commission for weeks.

Kobe taped it up. He couldn't even hold a basketball, let alone shoot one—that's how bad it was. But he refused to go on the IR (the Injured Reserve list). He didn't take even one day off.

Instead, he completely changed his shot. I couldn't believe it when I saw it.

Kobe's jump shot had always been unique. When he was expanding his game and adding the three-point shot to his repertoire, his summer practice routine included 1,300 *made* three-point shots a day. The form on his jump shot was as distinctive as a fingerprint. If you saw only the shadow of the shooter making the shot, you would know immediately it was Kobe Bryant. His arms went up, and after the release his fingers relaxed, drooping downward. His body, like a lightly drawn bowstring, smoothly curved backward in an arc. His legs, too, after the initial propulsion upward, relaxed; the feet, like his fingers, drooped downward, angled toward the floor.

He developed his jump shot in an intuitive way. It was something that came out of him and expressed itself. He didn't force it to be one way or another. It was unconventional. He was listening to his internal wisdom, the greatness within, which was saying to him: This is the way to do it. It is true that he had intention behind this. But it was an intention to allow whatever was unfolding to unfold. To allow life to speak for itself.

Being unlocked in this way is very subtle. What's important to understand is that it's about getting in touch and focusing on the inside instead of focusing on what's outside of us. So what's out there is a reflection of what's in here. That's when life starts to feel right. It takes on a rhythm and direction all its own, and we're amazed and carried along. Kobe through practicing came to that understanding: *This is how I need to do it. This feels right. I feel more alive. I feel more like myself when I do it this way.*

After Kobe changed his shot, the ball sat differently in his hands. His release was different. But he quickly and seamlessly adapted; even though the injury took some time to heal, he played through it, missed no time, and still shot a high percentage. Nobody does that.

I saw Kobe breaking out in real time. The similarities with Michael Jordan were already there. Both were vibrating at a different level, although it must be said that MJ was inimitable, unique in this regard, beyond anyone else I have ever seen, and that does include Kobe. There was a palpable force field around MJ. Nothing could shake him. Nothing could break that force field. It was extraterrestrial. It was supernatural. Kobe was miraculous—Achilles without the heel. But I'm not comparing Kobe to MJ anymore. Kobe was Kobe.

Kobe completely understood the level of focus and commitment it took me, as a recovering addict, to come from where I was coming from, understood my ongoing commitment to work it day in and day out with *no* days off. My commitment was and is total. The adage in AA's "Big Book" for recovery— one day at a time—was a mantra for both of us. Kobe was fanatical, obsessed, single-minded. He was all-in *all* the time. Just like me.

My support of Kobe was unwavering and unconditional. I worked with him on being in the moment, not being distracted. You could say I worked with him to develop what was already there—a poise, a remarkable ability to focus and concentrate and sustain a locked-in toughness. He understood the deeper intelligence inside himself and how it changed his game when he tapped into it. That deeper intelligence is what we worked on attaining.

SCORING WITHOUT TRYING TO SCORE

In early January 2015, I got a call from Kobe inviting me out to Newport Beach to spend a few days hanging out with him. Kobe was preparing for the next phase, the transition to life after retiring from basketball.

It was immediately clear, when I joined him, that he was at peace with leaving the game. I was impressed with his process and the ease he had around his decision. He was fully engaged with his company, Kobe Inc. I visited its offices and met the staff. Its creative wing would help Kobe win an Oscar for his animated short film *Dear Basketball*, and that wing was also responsible for the production of his autobiographical documentary *Kobe Bryant's Muse*, which would initially air on Showtime.

Kobe and I talked for many hours over the days I was there. He invited me to a Lakers game one night; we flew by helicopter to downtown LA, landed on a rooftop, and took a limo a short distance to Staples Center. Everyone at Staples gathered around him. They all wanted to be in his orbit. He had that kind of charisma, that kind of presence.

People said Kobe was arrogant toward his teammates. If they didn't have his level of commitment, if they weren't completely prepared and willing to do whatever it took to win, he would get up in their face. He was going to tell them exactly where they were sloppy, where they were falling down. It wasn't because he was arrogant but because he put in the work. Can you feel the difference? If he didn't pass the ball to you, it was because he didn't trust you. He made those calls purely on the level of instinct, of intuition, after watching all the tape, after all the endless practices and reps. He just let it all go at game time. He was a conduit, playing by feel. People wanted him to be humble. But that was not his way.

When I asked Kobe for a blurb for my book *The Mindful Athlete*, he wrote generously: "George helped me . . . to be neither distracted or focused, rigid or flexible, passive or aggressive. I learned just to be."

To just be. He summed it up in a nutshell. That really is the essence of all I teach. Kobe was able to translate that into the beauty of his game. He had transcended mamba. His playing was very simple, nothing extra. He moved like flowing water, with a sinuous power and an inexplicable grace. To just be was what I taught Kobe and what I try to impart to every young athlete and all the other types of people looking to up their game.

One of the last conversations we shared seems particularly poignant in light of his premature death.

"Do you remember the time I said to you that the best way to score is to not try to score?" I asked.

"Of course I do."

"You had sixteen points in the first quarter. It was like you weren't even trying."

"It wasn't me that was out there shooting. It wasn't me, and yet it was."

"That's how it goes when you're unlocked."

Kobe nodded. He had let loose his inner power, the special greatness within him. And now, when he was no longer an elite athlete, he had tapped into a profound peace in his life using that same set of skills.

TRYING WITHOUT TRYING, HOOKING INTO SOMETHING LARGER than ourselves—this was what I wanted to impart to young Khaleel. I wanted to encourage him, guide him, although perhaps not quite in the way he hoped. Kobe was a god to him, and here he was talking to a guy who had coached his god.

"You looked pretty good out there," I told Khaleel.

"Sure. Against those guys. Candy from babies. I know I could be a whole lot better."

"You're young. You have time."

"No, sir. I don't have time. I want it like Kobe. You gotta help me."

Many are called but few are chosen, I thought. But I didn't say that.

"What about becoming *you*?" I asked Khaleel. "Forget for a minute about Kobe. What about being true to *yourself*?"

He looked at me, perplexed, but I felt a distant shimmering.

"That power inside you that you want to unlock? It doesn't have anything to do with Kobe. It's your unique gift to the world. Find your authentic self. Find yourself and you will find the greatness you seek."

I could feel him quiet internally and settle.

"That's it," I said. "Now you've got it."

I could feel the force of Khaleel's energy shift.

Find yourself. To this great work, we *all* are chosen.

We stood together, looking at each other; all around us whistles blew, sneakers squeaked on the hardwood floor, and there was the *pat pat pat* of dribbling balls: practice was starting up again.

I broke the silence between us. "Kobe and I would often talk about imposing our will," I said. "You know how people say he 'imposed his will' on the game? I'm not just talking about Kobe here."

"People say that all the time."

"They do. But it's not quite accurate. That's not what it's about. Self-centered, competitively aggressive, worried about winning—some people saw Kobe that way. But that wasn't Kobe. And that's not the way we want to be."

Khaleel's eyes were shining bright.

"Our will is not some outside force that pushes and bullies its way to achieve a goal. It is generated from inside of us through awareness and intuition. This force is unique to us. When it's unlocked, it impacts everything and everyone around us—*this* is the way we want to impose our will."

I then told him the story of Kobe scoring sixteen points in the first quarter and how Kobe loved talking about the theory that the best way to score is to not try to score.

"Khaleel, we need you out here!" his coach barked.

"What should I call you? Coach?" Khaleel asked as he turned to go.

"You can call me whatever you want. Just don't call me late for dinner."

That cracked both of us up. Khaleel looked back as he ran toward practice. The smile on his face said it all. I felt the flow of energy between us, a spark of newfound understanding radiating from Khaleel. He was ready to begin his own journey.

BEING "BREATHED"

The best way to score is to not try to score. We perform better when we forget ourselves and just let it happen. The classic *Zen in the Art of Archery*, written in the 1940s by the German philosopher Eugen Herrigel, is a brilliant rendering of this idea. The book was very important to me as I developed my own style of teaching, and I have incorporated many of its lessons. The book contains profound wisdom that can take lifetimes to master; but we can draw some of the marrow from it and apply it to all areas of life.

One of the primary lessons that Herrigel learns from his archery *sensei*, Master Kenzo Awa, is to let the arrow shoot itself. This is the same thing I taught Kobe—to score without trying to score. Awa teaches Herrigel what in the Zen arts is called "effortless effort." The arrow finds a target not because we're trying to hit the target, not even because we're *looking* at the target. We cultivate being present and allow our inner wisdom to express itself.

The Zen art of archery in Japan is called "kyudo," the "way of the bow." In kyudo, the bow, six feet long, is held over the head, the arrow nocked into the bowstring, positioned parallel to the ground. If you visualize this, you can imagine that the long, stiff bow is tremendously hard to draw. And yet the drawing of the bow is of the utmost importance. It is primary, and it turns out that Herrigel's master can read everything about Herrigel and his life and level of attainment in this one act. In the same way, we can read everything we need to know about

Kobe in the drooping fingers and the tilt of his toes on his jump shot.

For the draw, Awa insists that Herrigel use only the strength in his hands. The arms, shoulders, and rest of the body must be relaxed. "When drawing the string you should not exert the full strength of your body," the master says, "but you must learn to let only your two hands do the work, while your arm and shoulder muscles remain relaxed, as though they looked on impassively."

For many months, Herrigel attempts to draw the bow in this manner. Through his futile struggles the master is polite, praising his effort and enthusiasm and giving him pointers. Yet it seems that no guidance, however well-intentioned, will enable Herrigel to be able to draw the bow correctly, with even a fraction of Awa's relaxed and seemingly effortless grace. Finally, Herrigel has had enough. Despite his best efforts, he has to admit that he simply cannot do it and gives up, telling Awa that he's been making a conscientious effort to remain relaxed during the arduous process of the draw; it is simply not working.

"That's just the trouble, you make an effort to think about it. Concentrate entirely on your breathing, as if you had nothing else to do."

Awa then teaches Herrigel how to breathe. This very deliberate, specific process involves forcing the in-breath down gently in the abdomen and holding it, and then breathing out as slowly and evenly as possible. By practicing this technique, Herrigel discovers that the energy he gets from breathing is circulated by the body in such a way as to allow the bow to be correctly drawn. It takes many months, but finally Herrigel feels that he loses himself effortlessly in the breath and at times feels as though he's not the one doing the breathing, but instead is being "breathed." Only at this point is he truly able to progress in the way of the bow.

Herrigel asks the friend who introduced him to Awa why Awa had waited so long and put him through so much torture before teaching him the fundamentals of the breath, without which one has absolutely no chance of ever being able to draw the bow, let alone shoot.

"Had he begun the lessons with breathing exercises," his friend says, "he would never have been able to convince you that you owe them [breathing techniques] anything decisive. You had to suffer shipwreck through your own efforts before you were ready to seize the lifebelt he threw you."

Learning to breathe is a crucial first step for what Zen calls the "artless arts," of which kyudo is but one. There is the art of the ink-brush and flower arranging and the art of tea and the martial arts. All are seen as vehicles of self-development and ways to touch ultimate truth, the real beyond appearances and delusion. All cultivate a naturalness, a grace, an ability to be fully in the moment.

In kyudo, as in all areas of life, energy has to build and be released at the proper time, in accord with rhythms to which we are not usually attuned. Herrigel gives the example of a clump of snow slipping from a leaf. The leaf bends and bends under the weight of the accumulating snow until finally the angle of the leaf tilted downward is so steep that the snow falls off and the leaf springs back. This is the way of the bow. The bowstring is released in the same way that the leaf bends and springs back. The timing of the release is perfectly natural. It is unforced. It is not intentional but effortless and inevitable.

In coaching Herrigel, Awa says, "The right shot at the right moment does not come because you do not let go of yourself. You do not wait for fulfillment but brace yourself for failure." How true this is in all we do. The predisposition toward failure can be subtle, but it is nonetheless deadly. And just as we started this chapter, the question arises: How can we move from bracing for failure to waiting for fulfillment? That's what this book will show you.

The kyudo master insists that "right art" is "purposeless" and "aimless." What stands in Herrigel's way to being able to do what Kobe did—to score without trying to score—is too much "willful will." And Awa adds an even more significant insight, one that we would do well to keep close and apply to all aspects of the way we live and relate to the world.

"You think that what you do not do yourself does not happen," the master says.

The implications of this short statement are profound. On one level, the master is pointing to a kind of narcissism that passes for everyday life. Something is important or significant only if it's happening to me. Everything else is somehow out there and not quite as important or real. I'm sure that many of us are familiar with that position. In fact, if we're honest, this is how we mostly live.

But the master is pointing at something deeper and even more significant. He says that when we do something, we think *we* are doing it. In one sense that may be true, but our involvement isn't *all* that's happening. Something is flowing through us that is much greater than we are. Our egos tell us that we are the person who does this or that. But we're not. When we are unlocked and in touch with the power within us, in touch with our true selves, we move in effortless synchronicity with the greater whole; life moves in us and through us. Which is what is going on all the time anyway, although we're not in touch with it, mindful of it, because our thinking process gets in the way.

The experience of living in the unimpeded flow of the energy of life is Herrigel's experience of being "breathed." It is the arrow loosed by the master with his eyes closed that unfailingly finds the target. It is two arrows meeting in midair. It is scoring without trying to score. It is being unlocked and finding the greatness within. It involves a deeper seeing and being, an awakening to our true nature and our authentic selves, and it is the embodied realization of our oneness with everything that is.

In the following chapters, you will learn how to access this boundless gift for yourself, fully tapping into the expansive power within you.

DESCENT

———

There is an illusion about America, a myth about America to which
we are clinging which has nothing to do with the lives we lead
and I don't believe that anybody in this country who has really
thought about it or really almost anybody who has been brought
up against it—and almost all of us have one way or another—this
collision between one's image of oneself and what one actually is is
always very painful and there are two things you can do about it,
you can meet the collision head-on and try and become what you
really are or you can retreat and try to remain what you thought
you were, which is a fantasy, in which you will certainly perish.

—James Baldwin

People have called me a "performance whisperer." I coax
and tease. I "whisper" to the stubborn, oppositional part
of a person that resists growth, that refuses to break old habits.
To unlock inner greatness, we have to crack that shell to
access what's underneath. It can be a difficult, painful process,
challenging our mind much the way performance training
stretches our body and the limits of our endurance. The

mental training I do with athletes, prisoners, teachers, college administrators, businesspeople, and others shakes us out of the familiar and puts us in touch with deeper aspects of ourselves.

One of the primary lessons of mental training is that we always—100 percent of the time—need to be moving toward our goal. And in order to do that, we need to be able to let go, and I mean *really* let go, of our mistakes.

It's not easy. Blowing a big deal, flubbing up a class we're teaching, alienating people on whom our fortunes depend, making a mistake that causes our team to lose—these mistakes can keep us up at night. They can stick with us. And it's an unfortunate state of affairs, because we can't correct our errors if we're still living inside them. I love the quote by Yogi Berra that goes something like this: The game of baseball is 90 percent mental. The other half is physical.

It's a cliché—but true—that mistakes are a part of the process, any process, in whatever field we're in. We can't develop without them. We can't improve. We first have to own our mistakes and then move forward confidently with a positive attitude, not letting errors impede our progress. It takes mental toughness to look at our mistakes honestly, to recognize them. If we let our mistakes affect us, causing us to lose confidence, we will keep faltering—our full potential will always be out of reach. We need the mental confidence to be able to make mistakes and learn from them. You will soon find that acknowledging mistakes is a critical step in moving forward. It is when we hide or run from mistakes that they keep repeating, making it certain that we don't improve or grow. Acknowledging and growing from mistakes is part of what I call "affirmative awareness."

AFFIRMATIVE AWARENESS

A lot of people hear the word *meditation*, and it sets off alarms. They automatically think of something touchy-feely and perhaps a bit self-absorbed. Robes or yoga pants, spas or retreat centers, an activity and preoccupation that's soft and weak-minded. Almost another form of consumption, where people are buying something to make themselves feel better. These impressions don't reflect what meditation is or what mindfulness is about; they're misconceptions. Still, they're so popular that they're part of the reason I often prefer to define mindfulness as affirmative awareness rather than as a kind of meditation.

We touched above on how affirmative awareness relates to growing from mistakes rather than letting them rattle us, shake our confidence, and put us into a negative, self-doubting place. Affirmative awareness goes way beyond this, however. It means being able to let whatever's in front of us speak for itself in its own language. And then being able to say yes to it and embrace it. Mindfulness is not just about creating space inside yourself to allow that to happen. It is not a negation. It *affirms*. It says *yes*. It is both an awareness and an *embrace* of things as they are.

Affirmative awareness doesn't deny or blame. It simply says: This is the way it is, and I can change it. I am responsible, and I can change the way I see things—how they impress me. Mindfulness reflects what is in front of it. It strips away the need to interpret, to push away that which the mind perceives as unpleasant or grasp at what the mind thinks it wants. It requires the opposite of weakness. It requires fortitude: the strength to not shy away from the difficult or painful but rather see those things as an opportunity to learn and grow, to find the strength inside yourself, to open yourself to more of life's limitless opportunities.

We learn in the affirmative awareness of mindfulness that we have to be able to be still. To engage with what's in front of us moment by moment. To let what's in front of us speak in its own language. To work with that rather than embellishing or interpreting based on our past experience or our fantasies about the future—that is, our regrets or hopes. There's nothing wrong with wishing or hoping—wanting to improve who we are and to change the world for the better. Those impulses are sacred and part of who we are as human beings. First, however, it is important to learn to be still and develop insight—to have the capacity and awareness to see things as they are.

We shall see that for the ability to consistently perform at our best, we need to develop integrity. Mental training is critical, but it must be rooted in integrity and wisdom, spiritual qualities of insight and understanding and a feeling of what we might call intimacy with life. I'm not a Buddhist, and I'm not a Christian. Or perhaps I should say I am both a Buddhist and a Christian. I'm also a Kabbalist, Taoist, Sufi, Sikh, and whatever else you might want to call me. What I teach draws from all of these traditions, and all of these traditions offer a teaching that centers around the process of unlocking—around realizing our own connection to the divine, around being authentic. If we're not in touch with our authentic self, what good is performance or success? It's ultimately hollow and sterile and leads nowhere. It is unsustainable.

Gestalt therapists Muriel James and Dorothy Jongeward, practitioners in a field of psychology that focuses on the patient's current life experiences rather than delving into the past to assign blame, concisely express the need for authenticity in their book *Born to Win*:

> Winners have different potentials. Achievement is not the most important thing. Authenticity is. The authentic person experiences self-reality by knowing, being and becoming a credible, responsive person. Authentic people actualize their own unprecedented uniqueness and appreciate the uniqueness of others. Authentic persons—winners—do not dedicate their lives to the concept of what they imagine they should be; rather, they are themselves and as such do not use their energy putting on a performance.

When we get in touch with our authentic selves, we transform and are transformed. Our performance in athletics, work, art, business, relationships—all aspects of life—changes. We unlock our uniqueness, huge reserves of energy, and the feeling of having found our purpose and direction: we know who we are and where we're going.

This is not a narcissistic journey toward self-gratification and selfish achievement. In fact, the transformative journey is not primarily about us. It has a wider impact. By its nature the energy we unlock and the direction it sends us in has to do with giving back to the world and helping others. The philosopher Martin Buber wrote: "If a man makes peace in himself, he can make peace in the world." In other words, when we express the truth of who we are, we become a force for good.

How can we access this authenticity? The process is simple, but it is rarely easy. It involves unlocking our potential and seeing opportunities in daily life where we can access it. But first there has to be a sense of urgency to pursue the level of sustained excellence that comes from contact with that true self; in other words, there has to be a reason for that true self to consistently and powerfully express itself. We have to have the will and the willingness. That may be a long time coming, and it may involve a descent into the depths of our own darkness and despair. Imagine being in a crack house one moment and then behind the bench at an NBA game the next, watching the guys you've coached attain the kind of authenticity described above, implementing it in their game and competing for a championship. When I look back, it seems to have happened in the blink of an eye, an effortless and instantaneous transformation. But in reality it was a protracted life-and-death struggle. It was as Jesus said: "If you bring forth what is within you, what you bring forth will save you. If you do not bring forth what is within you, what you do not bring forth will destroy you" (Gospel of Thomas 70).

It took everything I had to finally bring forth what was within me. Not bringing forth the greatness within was destroying me.

To varying degrees, this is true for all of us. For some, it may be ruining our lives, and for others it may simply be holding us back from our potential.

HIDING OUT

The tamping down of who I was began early. It manifested in the way I lived in a fantasy world as a child, shrouding myself in make-believe. I desperately wanted to escape reality. Before I could walk, my aunt and uncle weaned me on beer; and, when I was older and could toddle around the house, I occasionally sneaked sips from my father's omnipresent bottles of Seagram's whiskey. I was always altering my consciousness. That's one way I retreated. I also went within; I barely looked at things outside myself. I simply couldn't see. It's as if my eyes were closed, and I was asleep. I didn't even know that I'd been in a fantasy world until I got out of detox. It's then that I realized it was the first time I could remember that I had gone twenty-one days without entering a fantasy world or taking any kind of stimulant. And that included the years when I was very young.

I was fragile, a small and skinny boy. When I didn't want to go to school, I simply stayed home and played with my toy soldiers. I was on my own in my own little world. My mother worked at the fancy Tremont Street Parker House Hotel in Boston as an elevator operator in the afternoons and evenings, and she didn't get home until close to midnight.

In my clearest early memory, my many brothers and sisters were off at school and the house was quiet. My mother was asleep, and I was alone in the bedroom I shared with one of my brothers. I had pleaded with my mother to be able to stay home, and she indulged me. I was a sickly child, prone to severe allergies, which on that day were especially acute. After my mother slathered me with sticky, evil-smelling calamine lotion, giving me a temporary respite from the itching and burning, I lost myself in television. I often watched Westerns during the day, enthralled by cowboys and Indians. I particularly loved John Wayne as cowhand, marshal, or gunslinger in the Westerns, and also as Marine Sergeant John Stryker in *Sands of Iwo Jima*. In that film he's a tough son of a bitch with a heart of gold, and he dies at the end, before the raising of the flag. Stryker's death consumed me. Death stalked my little world. John Wayne was my hero and he died. My mother could not console me; she loved John Wayne too. I played with my toy soldiers, pretending to defend Iwo Jima against the Japanese. A cone of light illuminated the battle scene from above; all around was a dark void.

I've since learned that I'm an empath—that is, I'm unusually sensitive to the feelings of others. I now know that as a child I repressed the way I registered other people's hurt. The sadness and pain of the homeless devastated me. I watched how folks walked past people experiencing homelessness, as though they didn't care that there was a fellow human being suffering. They didn't even bother to *look*. Their indifference seared me. Pain and death were all around, coming from all directions. I felt the pain in my family without any sense of where it came from. I only knew we were hurting, and that hurt was a knife in my heart.

My siblings wanted to toughen me up, especially my two older sisters closest to me in age. They saw my sensitivity and wanted it excised. I've heard comedian Alex Edelman quip: "My father grew up in a racist part of Boston, called Boston." My sisters were well aware that this was the world I would face. Beneath the toughening-ups, I knew they really did fear for me. I was a skinny little Black boy in the ghetto covered in sticky pink splotches of smelly anti-itch lotion. I couldn't afford to be weak. How often did I hear: "*Little* Georgie, stop being so sensitive! Don't be a wuss. You're too soft."

I was so silent and introverted that when I was in second grade my school put me in a special class for speech therapy. My teacher thought I had a problem speaking, but that wasn't it. I just didn't want to talk. In my house, if you spoke up you got beat up.

One day, I told a teacher I worshipped that I was going to go to college.

"No, you're not," he said. "You'll *never* go to college."

This shattered me.

It seemed like an unimaginable cruelty at the time. Maybe he wanted to give me a reality check or perhaps he, too, just wanted to toughen me up. The reason never made sense and the casual statement continued to hurt for years to come.

If he wanted to make me stronger, it worked. A fire started to burn out of that pain.

MY RECURRING DREAM

I had a recurring childhood dream after watching *Abbott and Costello Meet Frankenstein*, a comedic chiller that embedded itself in my unconscious. In my dream, Frankenstein roamed the world—specifically, my neighborhood. He was a looming, malevolent presence with the strength of ten men. He staggered up Quincy Street in the dead of night, tore open the door of our house, and lumbered up the stairs, searching for me. I tried to run away but my legs seemed to not work properly; I had the slow, sludgy gait of dreams. I strained forward, toward some hope that was offered just beyond reach, forever unattainable, managing to somehow stumble down the stairs and out the back door, just beyond the monster's grasp.

I don't remember if I had this terrifying dream every night for a time, but it frequently recurred, and I'd wake up in the dark, heart pounding. Frankenstein represented the transience of life: John Wayne, my hero, shot through the heart on Pacific sands. The undead monster was barely alive, stitched together from corpses and animated by lightning bolts. He was a horrifying reminder of the omnipresence of death in life, of which I was keenly aware even at such a young age.

This awareness was sharpened by the precarious circumstances of our household. We were living on the edge, our parents always working to feed us and keep a roof over our heads. Whatever foothold in the American dream we had achieved felt as though it could be obliterated at any moment. Perhaps the Frankenstein dream formed around these feelings of impending disaster and my acute sensitivity to other people's pain.

Then the most amazing thing happened. When I was a little bit older, I watched the comedy series *The Munsters* on television. For some reason, as in the Abbott and Costello Frankenstein movie, the combination of comedy and horror was irresistible to me. In one episode of the television show, Herman Munster, the benign and lovable Frankenstein look-alike father of the family, played basketball, Frankenstein style. I laughed and laughed. And after that, the dream disappeared, banished from my psyche as though it had never formed.

"MEETING CLOTHES"

The pain in my family was generational. Both my parents had been sharecroppers from around Birmingham, Alabama. The way sharecropping worked, families were always in debt, never out from under the weight of the money they owed. This indentured servitude was an extension of the slavery both sides of my family had endured, although the details of their lives as slaves—like the when-and-where origin of so many other African Americans—has been lost. I know from Ancestry.com that my genetic makeup is over 80 percent West African. I come from Nigeria, Cameroon, Congo, Western Sahara, Benin, Togo, Ivory Coast, and Ghana. There are also bits of England, Scotland, northwestern Europe, Sweden, and Denmark, as well as a small amount of genetic material from the northern Philippines!

Which just shows how connected we all are. We are indeed one human family.

The family's memory, that of my grandmother and my aunts and uncles, begins in Alabama, where we rented land and grew tobacco and cotton and other crops. As a child, I thought Alabama seemed infinitely far away. I studied maps to make sure it was part of the United States. Was the skinny little boy covered in hives a real American? I wasn't sure. I was so unlike John Wayne, with his manly drawl and unshakable confidence. Nothing rattled him, and the breadth of his shoulders was as wide as the sky.

My maternal grandmother was the first in our family to leave Alabama and the first to move north. She settled in Boston, temporarily leaving her many children behind with extended family, knowing that the Jim Crow South was no place to raise a family. She could be walking down the street with her children, and if one of them misbehaved, a white person could beat them right in front of her and there was nothing she could do about it. If one of her brothers or cousins or any Black boy or man wore a white shirt and it wasn't Sunday, he could be tarred and feathered or even lynched. "You had to know your place in the South," my grandmother said. "And if you had a good job and a car, whites could have a problem with that. But the Klan never showed up around our house because we had a big family. There were too many of us so they stayed away."

It was true we had a big family, but it wasn't just that. My mother's cousins, that side of the family, were powerful men—

Mandingo warriors. In the dawning of my consciousness in the 1950s, I see them as giants. My empathetic nature picked up on their pain. They had come back from serving in the armed forces in World War II shell-shocked, bruised around the eyes, haunted by the violence they had witnessed and participated in. This wasn't the fantasy world of my little cone of light and the escape hatch I was always scurrying down. This was the reality of killing men and seeing them die and living in constant fear for your own life punctuated by episodes of terror.

By the time I entered the picture, my grandmother worked as a domestic and lived alone in a house that was on the way we walked to school. Like my mother, she'd had a slew of kids, many of whom ended up living nearby in the Boston area. My immediate family was huge. I had twelve siblings—and then there were my aunts and uncles and cousins, all from my mother's side. Yes, the men were Mandingo warriors, but how strong these women were! It was said that when my mother was sharecropping, she could pick more cotton than three men. She gave birth to thirteen children and worked full-time. She inherited some of her strength from my grandmother, a woman who'd had the courage to leave what she knew behind in the South and come to a new place and forge a life for herself and her children.

My grandmother was medium height with a stocky build. She always dressed well. Her husband, my grandfather, was an ordained minister. They had divorced before my grandmother's exodus from Alabama, and he had remarried and had more children. That part of the family were vague, distant apparitions.

My grandmother always had guns around the house, even with all of us kids around. She had grown up around guns, which were part of life in the rural South, used for hunting and protection. When my grandmother wrote me a birthday card—as she did every year—she always addressed it to "Master George Mumford." She was very spiritual, heading to the Southern Baptist church every Sunday in her "meeting clothes" and fancy hats (her "crowns"), and the spirit moved in her when she listened to Mahalia Jackson's gospel hymns.

My family's life fell apart after my father's drinking got so bad we lost our house. I went to live with my grandmother for a period of several months. I'm not sure why it was me of all the kids who was chosen to take refuge in her home. She was tough and kind, by then retired and hobbled by arthritis. Although she walked laboriously with a cane, her mind was still feisty and quick. She was a contained person of few words. When she did speak, she told you how she saw it. She came from another era, another way of life in the rural Deep South. She chewed snuff.

CAMELOT

There was a brief period from 1957 when I was five, to 1961 when I was nine, that was a kind of Camelot period in the life of our family, coinciding with the Camelot days of the Kennedy White House. My family was relatively intact. Somehow my parents, perhaps with the help of my older siblings and my grandmother, had managed to scrape together the down payment on a nine-bedroom house on Quincy Street in the Boston neighborhood of Roxbury.

In my memory, during the Camelot period all my siblings are there and everyone is pitching in. I see our "sitting room" with lots of family and friends sitting around, eating and drinking and laughing. There is a warmth and liveliness. Although there isn't any money, people want to hang out with us. Something in the liveliness of our family's life draws them in. I see these comings and goings and the greetings, and I hear the chatter and merriment and the sounds of little feet running.

In the clamor and hubbub of that Mumford circus, I was largely ignored. What was I thinking about? What was I feeling? I can't tell you. And yet, as I cast myself back into the past, I can still feel a piercing sharpness, perhaps because we lost it all.

How did it happen? I'm not entirely sure. Two of my older sisters married. Suddenly, they were gone, as well as my older brother Johnny. He enlisted in the Marines in 1960 for what would eventually turn into two tours in Vietnam. He was a fascinating dude, six foot two, two hundred pounds, able to walk the length of the sitting room on his hands. This cat was no joke. He was a marksman in the Corps, a sharpshooter. During one of his tours, Johnny was captured by the North Vietnamese. He caught a break: "You're Black like us," the Viet Cong said. "Why do you fight for the whiteys? You can go. But don't let us see you again or we will shoot you dead."

Soon after Johnny joined up, my older brother Bill left. He was
very close to my mother but had a battling relationship with
my father. Energy seemed to flow through my mother into
him; over the years he had acted as her surrogate and kept the
family together. Finally, he'd had enough of my father, whose
drinking had escalated over the years. Bill knew he needed to
get out and find his own life, so he moved away to a little two-
bedroom apartment on Westland Avenue in the South End, near
Symphony Hall.

Bill had wonderful parties in that small apartment. He matured
into an extraordinary man, self-educated and urbane, a
connoisseur of wine who spoke Italian and knew opera and had
rich white friends in Europe who were highly placed.

But everything started to fade to black around the family after Bill
left. Color tones that had had warmth and luster turned muted
and dull. We ended up losing the house. My father's drunkenness
was a constant. He was either raging drunk or hungover. My father
was known around the neighborhood as "Wild Bill" because of
his ranting, reeling behavior when under the influence. He would
go berserk, a man possessed. He worked on the railroad, although
I've never been sure exactly in what capacity. My impression is
that he was some sort of laborer. I don't think he was a mechanic,
although he was certainly capable, the kind of man who could fix
anything, having grown up on a farm: the workings of machinery,
plumbing, and carpentry were second nature to him.

My father was small in stature, about five foot six and slender,
with straight black hair. The word was that he had Cherokee

blood in him, but Ancestry.com says there's no Native American in *me*, so go figure. Whatever the case, my father's straight hair definitely distinguished him, and maybe it was a reason that he decided to become a barber as well as holding down his job on the railroad. He cut hair in the evenings at a friend's shop.

Both before and after my father's decline, I was close to my sisters. "Perform, Georgie Porgie. *Perform.*" My sisters would pay me to dance when their friends came by. I'd shimmy and shake around the sitting room to the top-forty radio hits played by Arnie "Woo-Woo" Ginsburg. They laughed and whooped and egged me on. I flipped, did handsprings, was a veritable rubber-band man. They paid me to do the dishes for them. I was a willing washer.

I make it sound grim, but it wasn't. I loved my sisters and they loved me. And that love continued throughout our lives. My brothers and I, and my friends from that time in my life, were essentially raised by our sisters. Our ability to form close and lasting relationships with women over the years is an outgrowth of our closeness to our sisters. I treasured my relationships with them.

The beatings I experienced as a youngster ended when Little Georgie grew a foot in three years and the flips and handsprings turned into hard drives to the hoop on the basketball court and crossovers that left defenders in the dust. I put my little toy soldiers away, and in the place of my sick days of make-believe I came to be on the basketball court. Not that my life was idyllic. I was on Darvon and other pain meds for frequent tendon and muscular injuries and for GI problems, which I know now came from stress.

About the time I took to basketball, I learned that under the influence I was as wild as Wild Bill. I yearned for escape from my own stifled interior. I was Jekyll and Hyde—a shy boy who suddenly felt less inhibited. But it was as Jesus said in that earlier-quoted passage: "If you bring forth what is within you, what you bring forth will save you. If you do not bring forth what is within you, what you do not bring forth will destroy you." I turned to drugs and alcohol as an escape, a way to blunt what was inside me that needed expression. My own path toward unlocking took me on a grand tour of hell. I sank slowly, inexorably downward.

Basketball slowed, to some degree, my descent. I didn't get high during the season when I was on the junior varsity and varsity squads. I was always injured, though, so pain meds were often in use. My knees ached to the point that sometimes I was hobbled, and my back was frequently in spasm. The varsity coach played me sparingly, off the bench, afraid to give me minutes. It was in the city pickup games where I truly excelled. I had great quickness and bounce. I thought the pain in my knees and back was par for the course. Nothing out of the ordinary; nothing I couldn't handle with the help of a Darvon or two. I gritted my teeth and played right through. I have to partially credit my sisters, who took me to my first basketball game, for giving me new purpose.

Looking back on my childhood and teen years, I see evidence supporting my claim that it's not by repressing our experience but by seeking to understand it that we can "bring forth" what is inside, unlock and find the greatness within. I don't want to leave you with the impression that I was in a fantasy world all the time, but as I mentioned earlier, until I got into recovery I had no idea that I was hiding out. As Martin Buber says in *The Way of Man: According to Hasidic Teaching,* "As in Eden, God is still calling to us from our hideouts."

After Adam and Eve ate the fruit of the tree of knowledge, God asked them, "Where are you?" In other words, where are you hiding out? This—hiding out—is what we do when we distance ourselves from our true nature. My whole early life could be seen as a system of hideouts, whether my make-believe world of toy soldiers or the needle I loaded up with junk several times a day and slipped into a vein. And I suspect you have your own hideouts. Human beings are always looking "out there" for happiness and fulfillment. We try to control the way things are so that they go our way. That's impossible! People act as if they're not going to get old. As if they won't get sick. As if they'll never die. Despite being bombarded daily with the impermanence of life, we manage to turn a blind eye and pretend that we're somehow exempt. As I write this, the closest sister in age to me, Evelina, who asked me to dance and paid me to wash the dishes, has just died.

I came to terms with death long ago. I see our lives on a continuum of energy and matter, and I know that we exist in another form after we die. What happens to us after death is not so important, though. The whole point of what we're doing here is to manage the here and now. And that means finding out what's true inside ourselves and expressing it.

What prevented me from expressing my true self and being authentic as a child? Perhaps a lack of affirmative awareness. It took many years of sinking deeper and deeper into addiction, until I eventually had to come face-to-face with the paradoxical fact that I couldn't keep using or I would kill myself, but also that I couldn't *not* use. The heroin felt as essential to me as food or water. It was as life-sustaining as the air I breathed. My quandary was a Zen koan, the seemingly unsolvable riddles that Zen masters use to bring their students beyond thinking, beyond the rational mind, to moments of awakening.

The great spiritual teacher and writer Pema Chodron writes: "We always have to change the channel, change the temperature, change the music, because something is getting uneasy, something is getting restless, something is beginning to hurt, and we keep looking for alternatives." That was my life—it is *all* our lives to one degree or another. Chodron continues: "We . . . try to get comfort and to distract ourselves [from being who we are]."

Being who we are. That is the task, whether we're Kobe or Khaleel. Our work is to bring forth what is inside us. By doing this, we find the lives that we are supposed to be living, that we actually *want* to live. One way to begin this process is to have the kind of attention that I wrote about earlier as affirmative awareness, which accepts the way things are—impermanent, always changing. Another is to let what's in front of us speak in its own language—to work with what's in front of us without tainting it with regret or hope.

In this way, we will begin to change. As poet Mary Oliver wrote: "Attention is the beginning of devotion." Devotion to what? To the present moment, to being in the now, which is always where we live, whether we like it or not. To the divinity inside each of us, which is our authentic self. As painful as it can be, and as frightening, we need to emerge from our hideouts. Can we find the courage and resolve to embrace with affirmative awareness— which is another way of saying with gratitude and love— whatever is right in front of us? This one precious life that has been given us? We are always being asked deep inside, moment to moment, "Where are you?" Are we able to answer, "Here I am."

Here I am. Right here. Right now.

HITTING BOTTOM

Hell is not punishment, it's training.

—Shunryu Suzuki

We all experience periods of isolation and loneliness, and there are times when our quest for happiness seems futile. How can we pursue our own joy when we are exhausted by what seem to be insurmountable problems in front of us? We may be plagued by addiction and feel caught, as I was, in an inexorable downward swing. We may be bogged down in a job leading nowhere. Regardless of our unique struggles, there are mental tools that can help us generate hope, that can give us the strength to come back into the flow of life instead of feeling as though we're in constant conflict with what is. My own journey through addiction taught me this lesson, and it's applicable to anyone searching for a way to feel hopeful and at peace, grateful for the life we have been given.

In college, I had kept my drug use secret from my basketball friends, and it would eventually draw me away from them; it

was only many years later, after I got sober, that I was able to
reconnect with them. Those years of distance and silence on
my part were such a pity—we had been so tight. That's what
addiction does: it cuts you off from the people you love and who
love you. It locks you up in a place where you're inaccessible and
unavailable.

During my junior year in college, however, my descent was just
beginning. Drugs were still something I could pretty much take
or leave. So it was no big deal when my friend Al Skinner (a
talented UMass basketball player who would go on to coach the
Boston College Eagles and hire me to work for the team) and
I drove from Amherst to Virginia in Al's little blue VW bug to
see our buddy Julius Erving play for the Virginia Squires. The
Squires team was part of the ABA, the American Basketball
Association (a league that had set itself up in 1967 as an
alternative to the NBA), which had signed Julius on a four-year
contract for five hundred thousand dollars to be paid over seven
years, a fortune in those days.

Dr. J, as he became known, had left UMass to join the league
because he needed the money and basketball was what he
wanted to do. Julius came from a family of modest means; the
money would make life easier and more comfortable for all of
them. When still at UMass, Julius, a scholarship student, had a
five-day meal plan. I was on a scholarship too—academic rather
than sports—which meant I was in the same situation. We were
on our own for meals on weekends. You know how it is when
you're nineteen years old and an athlete to boot: you burn about
a bazillion calories a day, and you're always starving. We had no

money and scrounged to feed ourselves on weekends. Julius had been promised an allowance to do his laundry and never got it. At other places, the boosters and alumni would come to games and slip the athletes money. Not at UMass in 1970.

The ABA contract was the opportunity of a lifetime, and Julius couldn't pass it up. He was going to play pro ball and eat as much as he wanted. Off he went to the Squires and the recently formed league with its red, white, and blue ball and its loosey-goosey, run-and-gun style of play. He bought a big house for eight thousand dollars with plenty of room for us to stay when we visited.

From starvation rations and a shitty little dorm room to a kick-ass mansion with a fully stocked refrigerator? We were there. We packed our bags, happy to give Julius the chance to show off his new digs, hang with our friend, and bask in the glamour of his stardom. Although Julius had dropped out of college to join the ABA, he would eventually get his degree fifteen years later from the University Without Walls, keeping a promise he had made to his mother. UMass eventually gave him an honorary doctorate. Damn straight. He has been ranked by ESPN as one of the twentieth century's greatest athletes.

When the ABA came calling, I was ecstatic for Julius. He had catapulted into the stratosphere of American life. At that time, there were fewer opportunities to make it as a Black man in the USA, whatever the field. Even in professional sports we still felt like we were slipping in through the cracks; we were the exception rather than the rule. As an example, before Al graduated from junior varsity to varsity, Julius was the only Black player on the UMass team. I remember the two guards he played with: small, compact white guys who would move up and down the court slowly, not a style that played to J's strengths.

Julius, on the other hand, was an ethereal talent, perhaps one of the ten best to ever play the game. In college, however, he was still a kid; no one knew what to expect in terms of the kind of player he would grow into.

Julius, Al, and I were three of the perhaps two hundred African American students at UMass Amherst in a student body of over twenty thousand. I don't remember any kind of overt racism or discrimination, but we stood out.

I had met Julius during orientation weekend. He was playing on an outside court on campus in his street shoes, dunking on people. Dunking on people in street shoes! Who does that? His hands were huge: he could dunk two balls at once, one in each hand. He grew three inches in college, starting at six three and ending up at six six. My freshman year we played basketball pickup games with and against each other and became tight. The following year, 1970, we roomed together, and we continued to room together until he signed the ABA contract.

Julius generated tremendous excitement at school. Students would line up hours before tipoff to gain entry to the Curry Hicks Physical Education Building (known as the Curry Hicks Cage), which was built in 1931 with a capacity of four thousand. On game days, it seemed like all twenty thousand students at

UMass were clamoring to get in. The games where Dr. J strutted his stuff were wild, infamous, over the top, becoming known as the "Rage in the Cage."

Dr. J was so far above and beyond that he simply couldn't be ignored. In his first varsity game, he scored thirty-two points and grabbed twenty-eight rebounds. He became an instant star. He couldn't go anywhere on campus without drawing a crowd. And he had tremendous charisma. Even in college, he was the Michael Jordan before Michael Jordan.

Little did I know that my connection with Julius was preparing me to work with Michael Jordan and other greats. It gave me the experience of being around greatness and learning how to help people with exceptional gifts and drive maneuver through the adulation and the isolation that being special, singled out, inevitably causes. It also started me thinking about the nature of talent and potential—where it comes from, why some people seem better at developing it or unlocking it than others, and how we might all be able to tap into our own latent capabilities, no matter who we are or what we do.

NO DETERRENT

When I drove down with Al to visit Julius in Virginia, I was on the cusp, not of greatness like Julius, but of sliding down the slippery slope of addiction. It was a slow descent through the levels of hell, which I now see as an essential part of the way I found the strength inside me, an essential part of what made me who I am today. It stripped me down to the nub. Addiction may not seem like it, but it could be thought of as a version of the hero's journey.

Joseph Campbell, the enormously influential author of *The Hero with a Thousand Faces*, brilliantly illuminated the archetypal hero's journey, which to one degree or another we are all on. The hero sets out from his homeland to slay the dragon, to save the kingdom and win the princess. Campbell's point, extrapolating from Jungian psychology, is that we *all* need to confront and, in one sense or another, slay our dragons, conquer the cave of darkness inside us where our fears and delusions live, before we can return home with hard-won insight, wisdom, and self-knowledge and take our rightful place. Only after this kind of painful and perilous confrontation will we truly have something to offer, to contribute to the world. That is what's most significant. Not just that you come to know yourself by confronting your dragons, but that through doing so you are able to help others, to make a difference.

This is not a once-and-for-all process. It is something that never stops. Imagine yourself as a phoenix, rising from the ashes of the dragon that has blasted you with fiery breath. You don't rise from the ashes complete and fully realized, your phoenix plumage all shimmering and aglow. No. You have to keep evolving. Part of being unlocked is that it is *not* a onetime deal. It really never ends.

I HAD BEEN USING HEROIN FROM THE TIME I WAS FOURTEEN, BUT I didn't start mainlining (injecting directly into a vein) until my junior year in college. Before that, I'd skin-pop, jabbing a needle into the muscle under my skin. My heroin use was progressive: from snorting, to skin-popping, and finally mainlining. Still, though, I used at my own pace. I could have junk around and save it for a month or two; I would just take one hit, kite around, and then leave it be. And I would not touch drugs during basketball season.

Then, in the fall of my sophomore year, I got hurt, couldn't play for a time, and the gloves came off. It happened in a second. In a campus pickup game, I was driving to the hoop, up in the air, when the guy who was guarding me came in underneath. I glanced off him on the way down from my leap and was immediately off-kilter, slamming down on the hardwood, my ankle a twisted mess. It was one of those injuries where everyone watching it happen gasped and shielded their eyes. I was down for the count: I couldn't stand, let alone walk. My teammates carried me off the court to the infirmary. I was in a walking cast for several weeks, which came off two days before varsity tryouts. I tried out for the team limping. It was a foregone conclusion—I just couldn't play.

The doctor treating me prescribed Darvon (yet again) for the more or less constant ankle pain. Darvon was cool, but heroin was better; it vanquished both the pain and the disappointment. The German guy who discovered it gave it its name because it was *heroic*. And so it is. And so it was—and yet ultimately catastrophic.

I began using more consistently during my senior year. At that point I had definitely developed a habit. I was Joe College by day: shy, buttoned up, diligent, a cat who was good with numbers and their pristine predictability—one plus one equaled two. In that calculation there was no pain or despair, no emotional quotient or dire implication. At night, though, I ran wild, slipping the needle into the vein, feeling the rush I craved, the ankle suddenly a distant memory, something harmlessly small, far away, and completely inconsequential. I swooned in voluptuous tactility and drifting poppy dreams.

It was a double life—a secret life. I kept that secret part of myself away from even Julius and Al. When I graduated in 1973, I lost contact with Julius. I was apprised of his status through Al for a while, until I stopped relating to Al as well. It would be many years before I reestablished my relationship with them, my dear friends. Al would hire me to work with the Boston College men's basketball team, as noted earlier, and Julius and I would eventually come back together. Distancing myself from them was one of the worst parts of slipping into addiction.

A CREEPING THING

I was what you would call a functional junkie. With my degree in accounting from UMass, I worked in white-collar jobs. I was soon a senior financial analyst, negotiating government contracts, doing cost control and cost reporting. It was a well-paying job, and its primary purpose—as I saw it—was to keep me well-supplied. I'd wake up in the morning, cook up some junk, sling a tourniquet around my bicep, and drive the load home.

My works went with me to the office. I fixed in a bathroom stall during lunch. And then I repeated the process at night—another hefty fix along with booze until my eyes fluttered closed and I sank into oblivion.

Addiction is a creeping thing. You think you have it all under control until you don't. We might think of it as a switch that moves between impulse and compulsion. One of my first Buddhist teachers, Larry Rosenberg, has an amusing anecdote in his book *Breath by Breath*. He says he loved Indian food, but it didn't agree with him. Every time he ate it, he was in heaven during the meal, but an hour later he'd feel just awful. And yet he couldn't help himself. Rosenberg writes:

> "That's it," I'd think. "I'm never going to that restaurant again." A week later someone would ask me for dinner, and I'd say, "Indian food? Sure. I love it."

> You know what will happen if you eat that food, but the craving keeps growing until you say, "I don't care what happens, I've just got to have that taste." Fine. But that is the same kind of decision people make with all kinds of harmful behavior: overeating, drinking, drug use, sexual misconduct. The list could go on and on.

In contrast to Larry's hunger for Indian food, I don't believe that the cravings I felt—cravings that I sought to satisfy with drugs and alcohol—were just a carnal appetite or even a way to blunt my existential pain. They were also a way of seeking, of getting beyond the bounds of my own ego. By loosening up what was tight inside me, they eased my sense of separation and made me less self-conscious. They gave me the experience of being able to flow out of myself and connect. When I started meditating, I had oddly similar experiences. I began to look at the self, and I found that what we might call the "small self," who we think we are, doesn't really exist. We can't find it. It's an illusion.

The illusion of that self—and the tyranny of that illusion—is responsible for so much of our suffering. That small self generally runs our lives with its constant cravings and aversions, its endless dissatisfactions and fantasies that attempt to make life other than it is. Buddhist meditation works to bring us toward a realization of our true self, in contrast to our small or egotistic self. The basic insight that is expressed in one way or another in many wisdom traditions holds true: in order to find yourself you have to lose yourself.

Heroin simulates that kind of dissolution and unity. It is a sure way to escape whatever pain—physical or emotional—we may be feeling. Dissolution and unity. An escape from pain. Beyond the merely physical component of being hooked, that's why I was shooting up several times a day.

Still, what was inside me kept calling, waiting to be unlocked. When I felt free, high as a kite and uninhibited, I was trying to touch that true self. I was just going about it in the wrong way. Junk can be a pretty good facsimile, for a while.

Finding the true self—that was always my calling. Where you come from doesn't matter. Where you've been? Come into the present. Come into the now. I tell the people I work with: Purify your mind and heart. You want to do that? Okay. Here's a way.

HITTING BOTTOM

For a long time, I told myself that I could use secretly and safely. No one would be the wiser. It would just be my thing, which I had under control, and it wouldn't bleed into other areas in my life. I refused to acknowledge all the warning signs that the drug was beginning to run me rather than vice versa. These signs can be sneaky. Such as I'm going to a party, and of course I can't go to a party if I'm not high. Or I had a tense day at work, and I'm not going to be able to get to sleep without a shot. And soon you find you can't brush your teeth—even the thought of brushing your teeth, let alone getting out of the house in the morning, is insurmountable without a shot. If you don't fix, you're soon dope-sick and crazed and you have to admit you're a full-on junkie who needs three shots a day just to feel something approaching normal.

That was exactly where I was when I'd used the same syringe so many times that its tip had weakened sufficiently to break off in my vein. I tightly wrapped a tourniquet around my arm and went to the nearest hospital. The ER doc said that had I not quickly applied the tourniquet, the needle point would have been sucked up into my vein and traveled all the way to my heart and killed me.

I "heard" what he was trying to tell me. *If I keep this up, I'm definitely going to die.* But how do you think about death when you're just trying to make it through each day without getting dope-sick or arrested?

The ER doc dug the needle tip out of my arm. For many years, I had a scar from that minor piece of surgery. Now, looking down at my arm, I see that age and time have erased it.

The doc treating me asked: "Are you interested in treatment options? You can get help for free, you know."

"Thanks, Doc, I'm good."

As soon as I was discharged, I beelined back to the shooting gallery. This time I used a fresh needle. I was no fool! I was not about to make the same mistake twice and ruin my high. A true dope fiend.

Soon I was sick and back in the hospital again, this time with an out-of-control infection that I'd ignored for too long. Junkies don't tend to sterilize their injection sites, and so shit happens. You're pretty much at the mercy of every little bacterium. So it was with me: high fever, hot redness at the tender-to-the-touch site, discoloration up the arm, exhaustion. In short, in rough shape—really *sick*. The kind of thing most people would have treated right away.

"If you keep going on like this, you're going to die," the doctor treating me warned, echoing the admonition of the earlier ER doc.

I was in the hospital for about a week. The doctors and nurses knew I was an addict, of course: track marks up and down my arms and symptoms of opioid withdrawal, which came on strong soon after I was admitted.

The nurses exchanged sideways glances. "He hardly has any veins left to draw blood from," one whispered. "Don't prescribe painkillers. Bet the next time he comes in here, it's straight to the morgue."

Dope sickness feels as though you've been laid low by a bad flu, except it's worse. Your body aches and you're racked by chills. The worst part of it is that you crave the thing you're missing: you know if you could only get what you need (and I mean *need*, just like you need food and water), you would be okay; you would begin to feel human again and things would be all right. Meanwhile, you're on the verge of turning into a hungry ghost and crawling through the streets, ready to sell your soul for a fix.

Finally, I could see how far gone I was, how desperate and helpless. I'd allowed a case of strep to spread into a serious infection. A bug that a toddler might easily overcome with cherry-flavored throat spray had brought me to death's door. I found myself in that existential catch-22 that has brought so many addicts to their knees. I couldn't keep getting high, but I also couldn't *not* get high. I didn't *want* to do another shot of heroin; it just didn't seem as though I had a choice.

KEEPING IT BY SHARING IT

Soon after my discharge from the hospital, on April 1, 1984, a friend and former get-high buddy, Danny, came by my house. He was clean now.

"Why don't you come to a meeting with me, George?"

"You mean like the old drunks do? *Hi, my name is . . .* With the gin blossoms around their eyes? I don't think so."

Then again, Danny looked healthy, relaxed, and strong. Not the jittery or glazed junkie with whom I had been familiar. Despite my skepticism, I found myself intrigued.

"How did you get clean?" I asked.

"One day at a time, brother. That's the *only* way."

He said he had entered a detox program to kick his habit and then attended AA meetings when he got out. Part of his recovery was doing the Twelve Steps, one of which requires reaching out to someone who is still using. That's why he came knocking at my door with the AA meeting invite. Danny had learned a lesson that would soon become key to my transformation: *The only way to keep what you've got is to share it.*

That principle applies to all parts of life, not just sobriety. It is one of my golden rules: I have tried my best to live my life by sharing what I learn. It's how I keep my heart open. In AA, you

give back to people you may know. You reach out and try to
help them, as Danny did, when they're at their lowest point.
They have to be willing to say, I've hit bottom: I'm ready to do
anything to stop using. That's where I was when Danny knocked:
I had hit bottom and there was no place left to go. I was ready.

After Danny dragged me to a meeting, I knew there was another
way, much as I hated to admit it. What can I say? Knowing there
was an alternative ruined my high. It was, indeed, as the Chinese
proverb that opens the previous chapter says: *To know and
not to do is, in fact, not to know.* Now I knew that there was an
alternative to getting high, and I couldn't *not* do.

I began reading the AA Big Book. I was on, then off the wagon.
Though I continued to drink and drug, something had changed.
Being high just wasn't the same. I listened to the ways in which
everyone in the AA rooms had had the same experience, which
I now recognized was also my experience. Their addiction had
destroyed their relationships and livelihood until life had become
unmanageable and there was literally no place left to go except
the grave.

When my fellow addicts talked about improving their conscious
contact with God, I was not put off. Perhaps it was because my
grandmother was so devout. The idea of surrender to a higher
power made me feel as I had in my early skin-popping days. I felt
a hunger. I wanted that connection with something larger than
myself. I wanted to be comforted and cradled and to find a refuge
from pain and anxiety, a place where everything felt good, seemed
as it should be; where I felt that life was fine and I was fine.

I realized that it was time to dig deeper. It was time to find out what was holding me back from being able to stop using completely. I found a therapist I liked. I knew that I needed to enter detox, but I worried that I could lose my job if it became known that I was a drug addict and alcoholic. The company where I worked had Department of Defense contracts, and I would probably be viewed as a security risk and fired.

My therapist and I came up with a plan that included a twenty-one-day detox program within walking distance of my house. I would enter the detox facility during my company's annual three-week manufacturing plant shutdown (when most people were encouraged to take time off) and use all my vacation days to get straight.

A MOMENT OF AWAKENING

As I walked to the detox facility on the morning of July 30, 1984, I had a realization. I remember thinking that the George who came out of detox could not be the same person who went in.

The detox facility butted up against the state hospital for the mentally ill; it was actually on the hospital grounds, right around the corner from where I'd grown up. The twenty or so of us in the program had a schedule of group therapy sessions and individual counseling. We were kept busy developing a concrete plan of what we would do and how we would live when we got out and weren't using. The staff helped us generate hope and then cultivated that hope inside us. Generating hope has become

tremendously important to me—one of the fundamental things
I teach.

I had been on a methadone program years before to try to kick
heroin. It didn't work: methadone only made things worse.
That shit gets into your bones. Try to get off it and your bones
ache. I knew that if I went into detox and took methadone to
help with withdrawal, I would emerge more addicted than I
went in. So I kicked it cold turkey. I had been drinking heavily,
and the staff was concerned that I'd seize without booze. I
carried a mouth guard so that if I did seize I wouldn't bite my
tongue.

The seizures, thankfully, didn't happen, but I don't remember
much else about those twenty-one days. It was like going
through a tunnel. What I do recall—vividly—is the experience
of *leaving* detox. That was one of the most significant days of
my life. I had a similar experience to the children of the Kogi
tribe in Colombia who are kept in a dark cave for the first nine
years of their lives. At an appointed time, they are brought out
of the cave into the light and the lush, green world. Can you
imagine that moment? What they must feel? At the very least,
an overwhelming sense of the beauty. These children become the
tribe's healers and seers.

Walking home along familiar Boston streets, I had a similar
experience: it was as if the world had been made anew.
Everything pulsed. The beauty of the ordinary dazzled me and
seemed inestimably precious. How could I have ever turned away
from it and squandered the miracle of my life?

I was indeed a different George. The fantasies and projections that I had used to make living bearable had dissolved, vanished into thin air, just like my Frankenstein dream. In their place reality, breathtakingly beautiful and exactly as it should be, beckoned. It did not need any adulteration or embellishment, and neither did I. For the first time in my memory, I felt that my life was truly my own. I didn't need to hide out anymore. God asked, "Where are you?" and I answered, "Here I am." I was filled with gratitude. I am no longer a slave to my addictions, I thought. I can make of my life whatever I choose.

True enough, but that choice had to be made again and again. I had three weeks' pay waiting for me on my first day back to work, and with that money in my pocket, the urge to use returned. My heart pounded; I couldn't focus on the numbers on the blinking screen. I rushed toward the office bathroom. For the past decade, almost every visit I'd made to those tiny stalls involved shooting up. Those stalls had been sanctuaries for a daily ritual. But that first day back to work, when I felt as though I couldn't take another moment without drugs, I opened the stall door, sat down, and repeated the Serenity Prayer: "God grant me the serenity to accept the things I cannot change, courage to change the things I can, and wisdom to know the difference."

Not only did it work, it was my first meditative experience, long before I knew anything about meditation. The Serenity Prayer was like a mantra that grounded me, that time and repeatedly, and helped the cravings pass.

The mental component of addiction never goes away. I knew that if I started using again I would be right back where I was when I entered detox—maybe not right away, but soon. I can't tell you how many people go back out after they've been in rehab, and they fix, OD, and die. The deadly opioid fentanyl has made this problem worse. In the compulsion to get high, you forget that you're buying something that's not calibrated. In those days, heroin was often cut with milk sugar or quinine. And if you cut it with quinine, it gives you an additional rush. I mean, I've got a PhD in this realm. You crave that rush. You need it in the same way that Larry Rosenberg needed the taste of Indian food on his tongue, although the compulsion for truly addictive substances such as drugs or alcohol is another order of magnitude: Larry wasn't going to risk imprisonment or death for a forkful of curry.

GRATEFUL MIND, GREAT MIND

My recovery has been about many things, but one of its most important parts has been generating feelings of gratitude and appreciation by taking nothing for granted and focusing on the positive. Plato said that a great mind is a grateful mind. To unlock the greatness within, it's vital that we're grateful.

Jon Kabat-Zinn, one of my mentors, was fond of saying: "As long as you are breathing, there is more right with you than wrong with you." That is an attitude of gratitude: we are grateful that we are alive and breathing.

Practicing gratitude often involves conscious effort. When I'm on a phone call to some company's customer service department, which can easily try one's patience (I'm sure I'm not alone here), I make sure to ask the associate to repeat his or her name at the end of the call, and then I say, "Thank you for your service. I'm grateful."

An attitude of gratitude is not so much about being grateful for specific things we have or don't have, it's more about a state of mind. I often talk about appreciating the non-toothache, for example. You don't really appreciate the non-toothache until your tooth is killing you; only then do you really appreciate the *non*-toothache. After a recent root canal, my mouth was a swollen mess. Just being able to chew now, being able to feel my lip, which is no longer swollen and numb—I'm extremely grateful. Small things like that, which we usually take for granted, can nevertheless affect us deeply.

Author Shawn Achor writes in *The Happiness Advantage* about cultivating happiness. We usually think of happiness as something that befalls us, he says. One day we wake up and—lo and behold—we're in a good mood. How did it happen? A rich uncle we barely knew dies and unexpectedly leaves us a million dollars. We're suddenly happy! Our child is about to graduate from college—we write that final tuition check and offer a silent prayer of thanks. Or the example from above: We have a toothache. We go to the dentist. He pulls the tooth. A few bad moments, but once it's out we feel immediately better. Relief floods through us.

These are all rather haphazard and transitory types of happiness. Sustainable happiness, Achor writes, is much more elusive. It is based on developing a number of different internal disciplines that train the mind, including cultivating gratitude. We can decrease anxiety and alleviate depression by thinking about three new things to be grateful for each day—three new things in each twenty-four-hour period. Achor suggests either writing them down or speaking them out loud.

Another practice I use to cultivate gratitude and promote sustainable happiness is catching yourself or somebody else doing something right. Be on the lookout for the ways people are contributing, enhancing, acting in positive, productive, supportive ways. Note that rightness out loud. Let people know you see their contribution and that it means something to you. Encourage people. Acknowledge effort.

If we practice gratitude, we're actually cultivating a great mind. And if we have a great mind, we're going to attract great things to us. That has been my experience. I go back to that philosopher Snoop Dogg, who says, "[I have] my mind on my money and my money on my mind." If I have gratitude on my mind, I have my mind on gratitude. If I have a grateful mind, I'm going to have a great mind. If I have a great mind, I'm going to attract great things to me.

Everyone's journey is different. Mine took me down a dark path with a bad outcome that was almost inevitable. Regardless of where you are—whether you're dealing with addiction, depression, anxiety, isolation, or simply wanting to improve your connection and engagement to life—keeping your mind on what is good, what is worthwhile, and what gives us meaning and purpose will enrich you.

The focusing of our mind and our attention is internal work and can be done regardless of circumstances. It's all about inner attitude. Instead of focusing on what's wrong and bringing that into our consciousness, we can control our consciousness by saying no to the negative and yes to the positive. In this way we invite our inner strength to become tangible and palpable within us. It is the strength of hope, fortitude, and courage. It lifts us up and connects us to the goodness of life. And most important, it helps us find ways to help other people feel that way too.

UNCOVERING THE MASTERPIECE WITHIN

Our deepest calling is to grow into our own authentic selfhood, whether or not it conforms to some image of who we ought to be. As we do so, we will not only find the joy that every human being seeks—we will also find our path of authentic service in the world.

—Parker J. Palmer

You may be familiar with what Michelangelo said about his approach to sculpting. He didn't actually create the statues for which he is famous; rather, he "released" them from the stone in which he worked. His process stripped away, laid bare. That is the process we all go through to unlock. We remove the extraneous, the layering of our conditioning and defenses, and the ways that we have been untrue to who we really are until we find what is authentic within us—an authenticity that is always there, waiting to be revealed.

I call this greatness inside of us the masterpiece within. We might also think of it as our essence. The people we most admire, who are accomplished, masters at what they do, are in touch with this essence.

But everybody has that masterpiece inside them. We need to uncover it. The degree to which we can see it and let it express itself is going to be reflected in the quality of our lives. The masterpiece within is ours and for no one else. It is always unique. There's only one; only one *you*.

As we've seen, one reason it can be difficult to access the masterpiece within is because of our very effective system of hideouts. We are proficient escape artists. We're not authentic; we're not present; we're not really here. And yet we have to be careful—accessing the masterpiece within is about more than simply being present. There's a wonderful quote by author Jack Kornfield that pops the balloon of just "be here now," of arriving at a state of "nowness" as though that were the be-all and end-all, the way to solve all our problems. Kornfield, a Buddhist teacher who wrote the classic *After the Ecstasy, the Laundry*, not only points to why we build our elaborate system of hideouts, he also warns us against the complacency and passivity of mere "presence": "You know, this idea of 'Be Here Now' and so forth, it sounds good. It's not so good. It isn't, because what happens when you're here now? . . . Pain, boredom, fear, loneliness, pleasure, joy, beautiful sunsets, wonderful tastes, horrible experiences, people being born, people dying, light, dark, up, down, parking your car on the wrong side of the street, getting your car towed; all those things. For if you live here, it means that you have to be open to what Zorba called 'The whole catastrophe.'" Kornfield is referring, of course, to Zorba the

Greek, the live-life-to-the-last-drop character in the novel by
Nikos Kazantzakis.

Zorba is a quintessential "seize the moment" type of guy. But, as
Kornfield notes, we miss the mark when we think coming into
the present moment is a panacea. It's what we do when we get
there that counts. The same holds true for the uncovering of our
inner masterpiece. Uncovering it does not lead into a state of self-
admiration and narcissistic rapture. We do not take our place on
a pedestal in the Uffizi for the whole world to come and admire.
On the contrary, the masterpiece is about action and expression.
It has to do with making a contribution and giving of oneself.
It requires that we whole-heartedly engage in life, with all its
bumps and bruises and ups and downs. It has to do, as Parker
Palmer says in the chapter epigraph, with finding "our path of
authentic service in the world."

THE MIND-BODY CONTINUUM

We all have a masterpiece inside us, and sometimes, as was the
case in my own life, the only way we can access it is through a
crisis, a moment of truth in which we have to make a decision
about why we're here and what we intend to do about it.

We are on a journey—the hero's journey we talked about in the
previous chapter—and we need help. Snow White had the seven
dwarfs: each dwarf made his own, unique contribution to help
Snow White on her journey. Alice, of *Alice in Wonderland*, had
the Mad Hatter to help her, a rather dubious helpmate but help

nonetheless. We are really never alone, although sometimes it can feel that way.

Acknowledging that I needed help, guidance, and support was a first step in the uncovering of my own masterpiece. One of the reasons I knew I needed help was that I was in physical pain. Once I got clean, the back pain and migraines that had been chronic for as long as I could remember asserted themselves with a vengeance. Chronic pain was part of the reason I had started using in the first place! Clean and sober, I wondered: How am I ever going to deal with the pain without medicating myself? What was the alternative? Was there one? I knew I couldn't go back on drugs or I would quickly become readdicted.

The migraines that hit me after I got out of detox were particularly awful. I could feel them coming on each time. They started small, just a little bit of tension and constriction, and then they built like a wave in the ocean or a fist slowly tightening.

Back pain and migraines led me to participate in a cutting-edge, out-of-the-box experimental program called Managing Stress. This program was run by Joan Borysenko, an extraordinary woman and student-colleague of Harvard professor Herbert Benson, who had coined the phrase "the relaxation response." Benson—an early pioneer in the field of behavioral medicine— studied what happens when our body, particularly our nervous system, relaxes. He described the relaxation response as a state of "rest and digest," which occurs when our parasympathetic nervous system is activated. Our heart rate and breathing slow; our blood pressure drops; we feel at ease. Benson compared that parasympathetic state to the way our nervous system works when we're in what he called our fight-or-flight mode.

When we perceive a threat, our sympathetic nervous system kicks in. Physician and integrative medicine expert Marilyn Mitchell describes the fight-or-flight response in an article on Benson's work in *Psychology Today*:

> The fight-or-flight stress response occurs naturally when we perceive that we are under excessive pressure, and it is designed to protect us from bodily harm. Our sympathetic nervous system becomes immediately engaged in creating a number of physiological changes, including increased metabolism, blood pressure, heart and breathing rate, dilation of pupils, constriction of our blood vessels, all of which work to enable us to fight or flee from a stressful or dangerous situation. It is common for individuals experiencing the fight-or-flight response to describe uncomfortable physiological changes like muscle tension, headache, upset stomach, racing heartbeat, and shallow breathing. The fight-or-flight response can become harmful when elicited frequently. When high levels of stress hormones are secreted often, they can contribute to a number of stress-related medical conditions such as cardiovascular disease, GI diseases, adrenal fatigue, and more.

The Managing Stress program that Borysenko ran taught us how to move from frequent fight-or-flight responses to what we perceive as threats to a relaxation response. She used meditative techniques that Benson had adapted from various traditions and that he used to promote healing. Borysenko taught us the connection between mind and body and how we could use our mind to regulate the body's processes and thereby collaborate with professionals to take control of our health and well-being, a term that's more encompassing than just the absence of illness and indicates our capacity to thrive.

Borysenko was a dynamo—a brilliant, attractive, tremendously warm and caring woman who was passionate and engaged. You can imagine my response to her, fresh out of detox, reborn but reeling, fragile and broken open: I was smitten. (I wasn't by any means the first person to have this response to Joan.) We would become good friends, and what a stroke of good fortune it was to find her so soon after getting out of detox. I needed an angel to help me through, and there she was. Just like the Mad Hatter or those dwarfs.

Joan knew whereof she spoke. She had used the mind-body continuum to heal herself from various stress-related disorders. I found her personal story inspiring. In her earlier life, she had been overworked and often ill. In her book *Minding the Body, Mending the Mind*, she writes movingly about her own downward trajectory as a young researcher:

> When I was twenty-four I was working on my doctoral dissertation at the Harvard Medical School, investigating the way cells maintain their attachment to one another. I was living on coffee and cigarettes, broke and tired, trying to cope with a troubled marriage and an infant son for whom I had far too little time. Furthermore, I was a relentless perfectionist, trying to control and succeed at everything. My emotions were

in an uproar, and anxiety and irritability were my constant companions.

I was also a physical wreck. Troubled by migraines all my life, I . . . added crippling stomach pains and vomiting to my list of psychosomatic illnesses. . . . I came down with bronchitis four times in two years . . . and developed high blood pressure.

Joan's marriage fell apart, and she was diagnosed with a spastic colon and treated with medication that didn't really work. The field of mind-body medicine was just beginning to form; there weren't holistic or alternative therapies available. A friend turned her on to yoga and meditation, and she slowly began to claw her way out of the morass of what she came to understand as *stress-induced* illness.

Meanwhile, Herbert Benson was simultaneously engaged in refining and expanding the process that Joan had explored to heal herself, looking at the ways our mind can create the conditions in our body; and, more broadly, how the mind creates the world we inhabit. Eventually Benson, Borysenko, and their colleague Ilan Kutz would found Boston's Mind/Body Clinic.

That philosophical truth—that the mind helps create the world we inhabit—is important. At the beginning of my recovery, however, I just wanted to find a way out of pain and learn how to cope with the stress of living in the world without the buffer of booze and drugs. Joan's Managing Stress program helped me do that by teaching me meditation techniques and helping me understand the mechanisms of stress and the effect my mental state had on my physical being.

Joan writes: "A subject under hypnosis raises a very real blister on her skin, even though the 'hot iron' the hypnotist says he is touching her with is, in reality, an ordinary pencil. In a clinical test, one third of women receiving a placebo instead of chemotherapy still lose their hair." In other words, our minds—our thoughts and beliefs—have a degree of control over our bodies that we are rarely aware of until we start to consciously and deliberately direct our attention.

There was a syllabus for Joan's stress management class at the clinic. I read all the books on it, as well as many of the other books that were referenced in those books—books on health, healing, psychology, and spirituality. This began my regimen of reading one book a week, which has continued for almost forty years.

MAKING A CONTRIBUTION

What I began learning with Joan has been at the root of everything I teach, whether I'm coaching athletes or MBAs. I learned to control the involuntary responses in my nervous system: I could affect my blood pressure, pulse, and respiration by directing my attention in a particular way. I began to understand and be able to trace in myself how my autonomic nervous system functioned and the ways I had used substances to evoke a facsimile. Drugs and alcohol can hijack our natural ability to generate the relaxation response. They're not the real thing, and—as users learn all too quickly—they're lousy imposters. They imitate the parasympathetic rest-and-digest state, but they're blunt instruments. They subvert the body's natural wisdom—your natural high, your natural ability to release endorphins (in just the right amount) that enable you to relax.

There are distinctions between left brain and right brain. I'm right-handed, so my left brain dominates most of the time. It's the controlling, planning part of the brain. The right brain, on the other hand, is nonlinear and creative. We could think of the left brain as more rational and the right brain as more intuitive, although current neuroscience suggests that the two parts of the brain aren't so distinct after all. But to simplify—one side of the brain is all about sequence, one plus one equals two, read chapters one through ten in order. The other side says, Jump in anywhere and one plus one might equal six if we would only give it a chance and view it in the right light. Joan showed me how to use my *whole* brain. I learned to do that through directing my attention.

Joan introduced me to the idea of "awfulizing," which is the tendency to see things through fear and doom, exaggerating how bad circumstances are and expecting the worst. We all have this outlook to a certain extent—it's a very human tendency, to which I was certainly not immune. I often thought that the worst was going to happen, and I exaggerated the difficulties of my situation with substances. That was no longer an option, if I hoped to gain physical and mental health. "Awfulizing" provokes the sympathetic part of the autonomic nervous system, bringing us into a state of fight or flight and the stress that goes with that kind of arousal—exactly the kind of stress I needed to avoid.

At the Mind/Body Clinic we were taught to counter "awfulizing" by directing attention to the breath. We learned full-body-scan techniques, breathing in while tightening each part of our body, starting at our toes. That's a great practice that we can try right now:

> Breathe in slowly and deeply and tighten your toes, bringing your attention and the awareness of the breath into your toes as you tighten them. Breathe slowly out and relax the toes. Breathe in and tighten your calf muscles. Breathe out and relax your lower legs. Do that slowly for all your different body parts up through your eyes and head.

This is a very effective way to induce the relaxation response. I hope you can feel the immediate difference in your body and mind.

The more time and energy we put into bringing the autonomic nervous system into the parasympathetic mode (inducing relaxation), rather than having it churn constantly in fight or flight, the more we will move toward higher levels of wellness. During stress—fight or flight—our various systems become overwhelmed with what we perceive as demand. Soon the demand seems to be for more resources than we have, and so this process builds. As we use relaxation methods to go toward higher and higher levels of wellness, when stress happens (as it inevitably does), we have a cushion and the stress doesn't overwhelm us and cause psychosomatic reactions.

Dealing with my chronic pain and through my reading, I learned to listen to my body, and the body doesn't lie. It is always talking to us, perhaps softly and subtly, but loudly and directly when we're in pain. As I learned to "follow the breath," I developed more sensitivity and began to be aware of my migraines coming on early, detecting them like storms still far out at sea. I began to see that the migraines were telling me something—usually that I was doing too much and needed to step back, slow down, and take some time to rest and digest. When my back acted up, it was giving me the same message: slow down; take some time. I stopped being in denial about being stressed. We like to think we can handle life, whatever it brings—that we're stoic and strong. I eventually stopped pretending that I was invincible and could handle anything and everything. None of us can.

One of the ways we generate unwanted stress is that the brain confuses what we actually experience with what we only think or imagine. We can have pain from the past and keep relating to it as if it were in the present; we keep reexperiencing it through stimuli that invoke it. This conflation was on vivid display when I went to the dentist early in my wellness journey. Because I had been a junkie for so many years, my gums and teeth needed immediate care. Self-care? Not a junkie's priority. An important part of my recovery was starting to take care of myself. I went to the dentist and found out, no big surprise, that I needed multiple fillings and root canals. When I was in the dentist chair, I noticed that as soon as I heard the sound of the drill, my body flinched, tightened up, and I felt that awful kind of squiggly hot nerve pain. I contracted. Yet when I relaxed, I realized that the sensation of the drill wasn't really pain: it was more a kind of pressure, and I could just experience it as such.

You can try this yourself with pain. Instead of labeling it as pain and reacting with an adverse conditioned response, try to experience it more as just sensation in the body. Don't make more out of it than it is. Work on trying to relax and breathe through it. I've found in my own grappling with pain that I can often diminish the sensations by relaxing.

Tuning into my body, I noticed we tend to see pain as a constant. But that's not really the case with pain. It can seem more or less constant, but it's not. There are actually many moments during days we view as painful from start to finish when we're not in pain—we just don't pay attention to those moments. After all, when pain is gone, it tends to be quickly forgotten, a remarkable feature of human experience and, we might say, of life in general.

I learned how to manage pain by embracing it. Sometimes the pain became so severe that I had to take medicine. But those instances became increasingly rare. I was mostly able to deal with the pain by listening to what it was telling me, which was more often than not that I was overstressed and needed to dial it back.

What, you may ask, was I so stressed about? Hadn't I just been born again? Wasn't the world new, fresh, and beautiful? Didn't I revel in freedom from addiction and rejoice in what I felt were limitless future possibilities? Yes! That was all real and true.

Still, life is complicated, as Kornfield notes in the quote above. I was waking up to what my life actually entailed. By not caring about anything but getting high, I had managed to accumulate a pile of bad debts. I was faced with paying bills too long ignored. I hired an attorney to help with this process, creating payment plans and seeking to right myself in the eyes of the world. I also began making amends to people I had hurt and disappointed. These moves were part of the Twelve Step program, and—as my brothers and sisters in recovery know—it's no cakewalk. Making amends brings up intense shame and self-doubt. Adding to this stress was what was happening at work. As I mentioned earlier, my work with Defense Department contracts required security clearance. If the company learned I'd had substance abuse issues, I would lose my clearance, which meant I would be fired. I felt as though I were waiting for the sword of Damocles to drop, living a lie, presenting myself as someone other than who I was. I was in disguise, even in some ways literally. For example, I had to wear long-sleeve shirts all year long to conceal the track marks up and down my arms. (These took years and years to fade and finally vanish.) The stress of living this double life often spiked. It sometimes seemed unbearable, and the urge to use rose inside me like a dragon.

As part of my junkie descent, I had managed to lose my car. During recovery, I rented cars to get to and from work, and I was working overtime, trying mightily to dig myself out of debt. At the same time, I had to go to thirty Twelve Step meetings in thirty days, sixty meetings in sixty days, ninety meetings in ninety days. I would often go to six meetings on weekends just to fit them all in. And I had to be constantly vigilant—

the addiction was still alive and kicking inside me, pushing my buttons. I was still in the same neighborhood where I had scored and used, living in my same house that had been my own private shooting gallery and open bar where it was always happy hour. There was the constant potential of slipping and taking a drink. I mean, why not? One drink! For God's sake, how could that hurt? The stress of a possible relapse pressed on me, day by day, sometimes moment to moment. And through all this the migraines swept in, swamping me with such excruciating pain that I couldn't keep my eyes open.

Keeping clean and staying sober took everything I had. I did give it up to the "higher power," however we want to think of that, in the parlance of AA. This kind of commitment and dedication to sobriety became part of me. I was grappling with my demons on my hero's journey to uncover the masterpiece within. This battle-tested state would eventually allow me to relate to all individuals going through their own battles–whether that was someone incarcerated or an NBA superstar. With Kobe, he immediately knew that we were kindred souls—single-minded, with unwavering focus. He recognized me as I recognized him— the respect flowed both ways.

In those early days of my recovery, I committed to learning, committed to my sobriety, committed to what I felt awakening inside me, committed to discovering who I was beyond my hideouts and delusions. The freedom and joy I felt in being clean was undeniable. The masterpiece within was glimmering deep inside me, waiting to be revealed. It beckoned, inviting me to uncover it.

I realized that it not only wanted to be seen—it wanted to make a contribution. This was a terrifying realization. I had been so dishonest. How could I become real with people? My purpose *had* been to get high—and to keep getting high. Now I wanted to contribute. I took the Christian gospel's primary commitment to heart: *To love you, God, with all my heart and soul, and to love my neighbor as myself.* I knew that I had failed miserably at both. I had been selfish, self-centered, and narcissistic. I hadn't worried about what was going on with anyone else. I hadn't been interested in good deeds. I had just been stuck on *me, me, me.* Getting high—there was no room for anything else.

Einstein said that the most important decision we have to make is whether we believe we live in a friendly or a hostile universe. When we believe that the universe is unfriendly, we are always in fight-or-flight mode. It is impossible to grow in those conditions. We need to be able to open ourselves and take in and be curious. We need to digest. We can't be in survival mode and growth mode at the same time.

I so desperately wanted to grow. I wanted to learn. I knew that I needed to take responsibility for this desire to understand myself and how the world works. My commitment to learning has helped me in this new way of being, of investigating and training myself. It appealed to the athlete in me, the mental training that focused on learning how to read the language of the body, the discipline of being able to use my mind to affect how I felt and being able to start guiding my life. It was through the clinic and Joan that I was introduced to the Insight Meditation Society, which had a center in the rural area of Barre, Massachusetts. Joan urged me to go there on retreat, and away I went.

FINDING THE PATH

The Insight Meditation Society, or IMS, was stuck up in north-central Massachusetts, literally in the middle of nowhere. For a dude like me who had been born and raised in the city, being there was an odd experience. Where were all the people and houses and cars? Why was it so *quiet*? Did people actually live here? It seemed unlikely. What did they do? Trees, yes—there were a lot of them. And birds. But people? *Really?*

I was out of place: a city dude in a green emptiness, adrift in what I guess you could call *nature*. My sense of displacement was only heightened by the way I stood out among the uniformly white students and staff. At that time, and still a bit to this day, Buddhist communities in the United States were bereft of minorities. The Buddhist world catered to well-educated, well-heeled white people who were looking beyond their religion or cultural traditions for wisdom from the East. The lack of diversity didn't bother me. I was all about what IMS was teaching. It had been founded by Sharon Salzberg, Jack Kornfield, and Joseph Goldstein, and they used Buddhist wisdom and meditation techniques not only for the pursuit of enlightenment but more broadly for health, as a way to handle stress and live a happier, more balanced and productive life. They combined psychology, Western medicine, and academic training with Buddhist teachings and philosophy.

The one-week retreat was silent—no talking at all! At 5:30 a.m. we began hour-long sessions of sitting meditation in the light, airy meditation hall. These were followed by periods of walking meditation and *seva*, or service. Each day was punctuated by simple meals, eaten in silence. There were talks in the evening, given by my first teacher, Larry Rosenberg, a Brooklyn Jew with a PhD in social psychology who came from generations of rabbis and had taught psychology at the University of Chicago and the Harvard Medical School. His talks were infused with wry Jewish humor: he loved to joke. Which was just what I needed to help give myself over to the practice. The daily schedule ended with lights out at 10:00 p.m.

SITTING MEDITATION WAS A STRUGGLE FOR ME, AS IT IS FOR A lot of people. It was painful to sit cross-legged, and even when I transferred to a chair (which is a perfectly acceptable alternative), my mind churned a million miles per hour. It churned about everything and nothing. I fell into deep holes of self-recrimination and regret. I looked for illumination, but mostly what I found was chaos and darkness. Frankly, it was torture. Nonetheless, I was committed. Nothing was going to stop me, and I worked through it. I wanted to investigate. I was curious, a true seeker (God help me!). It wasn't even voluntary, really. There was something pulling me that I was powerless to resist. It was like a riptide. They say when you're caught in such a tide you have to swim with it. You will exhaust yourself trying to swim against it, trying to break free from its pull. That's how people drown. I didn't always take that sage advice, of course. When sitting meditation was particularly hard, I took comfort in the words of the renowned Buddhist teacher Ajahn Chan, who said that when you get uncomfortable and you feel as though you want to quit, that's when you know you're finally getting somewhere.

Walking meditation provided ballast to the torture of sitting myself down. Walking was easier for me; it was physical. The mindful practice of following the breath, being in the body, putting one foot in front of the other, and staying conscious and present made perfect intuitive sense. You just walked. You kept your mind on your walking. You walked intentionally—that is, with the full intention of just walking, lifting your foot, moving it through space and down onto the ground. You can practice this yourself the next time you're walking. Really become conscious of what you're doing with your feet and the sensations in your feet and in your whole body as you take each step. That's all you need to know to practice, whenever and wherever you are. Coming back into your body with each step brings you out of your head and away from the constant static of what are mostly discombobulated thoughts.

Walking meditation was a powerful way for me to slow down and just do what I was doing without worrying about what I did yesterday or what I was going to do tomorrow. Man, did I need that! Walking meditation allowed me a glimpse into the still point at the center of our being, what I would come to call the "eye of the hurricane." This became a crucial component of what I would teach athletes and others—how to find this still, calm, quiet place when all around the storm rages. When we access this place, we can begin to organize ourselves. We can deploy our rational mind to see things in their proper perspective, to stop taking everything personally and let life be as it is; with that comes the ability to see how to do good and be compassionate, generous, helpful human beings. This is called "right view" in Buddhism. If you have wholesome thoughts, you're going to have wholesome actions. Mahatma Gandhi has a lovely formulation for this: Your beliefs become your thoughts; your thoughts become your words; your words become your actions; your actions become your habits; your habits become your values; your values become your destiny.

I knew Larry not only through that first IMS retreat but also through the Cambridge Insight Meditation Center (CIMC), which he ran and where I lived for a number of years. Larry was a tough teacher. He was always pushing me out of my comfort zone and taking away the things to which I was attached. I studied closely with him. Not only did he push me out of my comfort zone, but he was incredibly generous, and it was at his prompting that I was able to radically change the direction of my life.

One day, after practicing at the CIMC for some time, I went to the Center for meditation and then for my weekly private interview with Larry.

When I sat down in the interview room, Larry took one look at me and said, "George, you seem happy today."

I admitted to him that I had taken the day off from work.

"You should do that more often," he said. He made it sound as though it was one of his jokes, except it wasn't.

Soon after, he said, seemingly out of the blue: "George, you should do a three-month silent meditation retreat."

I was incredulous. "I can't afford it."

"I'll pay," he said.

That really made me think. (I ended up doing the retreat—at Barre again—but paying for it myself.)

Larry guided me to give up my attachment to my old way of life, the stability and money inherent in it—an attachment I felt even though it was completely uninspiring. I would eventually leave my job and become one of three residents at the Cambridge Insight Meditation Center.

The biggest thing Larry had me do to get me out of my comfort zone was teach.

"George, I want you to become a teacher here at the Center," he said to me one day.

"I don't want to teach!"

"That's why I want you to do it."

"Why? I don't know anything!"

"Think of it this way—to learn it, you have to teach it. The best teachers don't teach because it feeds their ego," Larry said.

"They're not full of themselves. They're not know-it-alls. They teach out of service."

This got me thinking. I had to admit I was a shy, introverted person, except when I was drunk or stoned—and *that* wasn't an option. When I first started speaking in public, I would stand up in front of the room and just shake. I had to tell myself, Okay, I shake. I'm going to be a shaking fool. So what? I came to see my motions as nothing more than energy moving through me. And that acceptance of myself eventually calmed me. I learned to channel that energy, to direct it, to flow with it and through it, and to let it express itself through me. As I attended to it, it pointed me toward the masterpiece within.

That took a while and it wasn't easy. Larry saw my shaking, rattled, discombobulated performances as a breaking down of who I thought I was, a stripping away. He saw through all that to my authenticity, who I really was. "Just follow that," he told me. "You'll see. It will be okay." I wasn't sure, but I persisted. He was my teacher, after all.

To embrace what we fear. To work through it. Is there a more powerful experience in life? This is, indeed, the hero's journey.

TO STUDY THE SELF IS TO FORGET THE SELF

I've had a number of remarkable experiences during meditation. One in particular sticks out in my memory. I was sitting in the CIMC. It was very different from meditating in Barre, in the calm, quiet countryside with all its trees and birds and the rest of nature, which I had made peace with and grown used to and even come to really enjoy over the course of many weekend and longer retreats.

The CIMC was in the middle of Cambridge, just off Central Square, a densely populated and heavily trafficked area. The hustle and bustle of Cambridge rattled and hummed within earshot of the Center's meditation hall through the day and into the night. During my extended stay there, I lived in a bedroom on the second floor with the other residents. Larry had an apartment on the third floor, from which he'd descend during the day to teach and oversee the place, and to which he'd retire at night. With his academic chops, keen intelligence, and winning humor, he was the kind of dude who could have done practically anything with his life; yet this simple, monkish existence of largely selfless service was what he had chosen. He was an inspiring example of what really gives life meaning and where true happiness is to be found.

Although you could hear the pulse of the city in the Center's meditation hall on the remarkable day I'm remembering, the room was clean and calm, smelling of incense and serenity. It was early on in my residency, and I was sitting with a group in the hall one morning. We were lined up on cushions and in chairs around the room. There were maybe fifteen or twenty of us. I was faintly aware, as I often was, of the nonstop racket happening a block or two away in Central Square, in contrast to the oasis of contemplative calm within the room.

I remember looking at the forms of people silently sitting, and then I closed my eyes. When I opened them—I think it was just a short time later—everyone had vanished: *there was no one there.* Can you imagine? I understand this experience as getting beyond the sense of self, gaining direct insight into the true nature of reality, where there is no difference between you and me, us and them, subject and object. As the great thirteenth-century Zen master Eihei Dogen wrote: "To study the self is to forget the self. To forget the self is to be awakened by the ten thousand things."

The awakening of the ten thousand things is another way of describing the experience of nonself, of becoming unlocked, of glimpsing the masterpiece within.

NO STRUGGLE, NO SWAG

After I had been clean for about two years, I went back to school and got my master's degree in counseling psychology from Cambridge College. Part of discovering the masterpiece within was recognizing and letting myself be moved by my hunger for intellectual stimulation.

My graduate degree exposed me to some of the great thinkers in religious existentialism: Paul Tillich, Martin Buber, and Viktor Frankl, among others.

Being and becoming *are* really one and the same. As philosophers and religious thinkers have said, from the Buddha to contemporary bestselling author and spiritual teacher Eckhart Tolle, there is no existence outside the now. The past is gone and the future has yet to arrive. We live in the moment, and yet we are so often lost in memory and regret or in fantasies about what our lives might or could or should be.

As Kornfield notes, living in the present and being in the moment doesn't mean we're in a constant state of bliss. Kornfield is a realist. Hear him again: "Pain, boredom, fear, loneliness, pleasure, joy, beautiful sunsets, wonderful tastes, horrible experiences, people being born, people dying, light, dark . . . the whole catastrophe." Which includes our existential loneliness and pain.

Let's circle back to a concept that we touched on in the previous chapter: the small self. Buddhism attributes feelings—I would call them insights—of loneliness and pain and the anxieties and sadness they provoke to the small self, the ego, which sees itself as separate and autonomous and is always trying to impose its will. Crucially, that small self is unwilling to accept impermanence, the transience of life and the inevitability of death. A buddha has awakened to intimacy with all things. Yet our separateness and loneliness are also real, as much a part of the human condition as our capacity for the realization of our interconnected nature. Could one of these aspects of human experience really exist without the other? Is one truer than the other?

To accept this reality as it is—that is the task. I have an acute awareness of our existential loneliness and pain and how strong the urge is to assuage it. My quest to slay my dragon and uncover

my greater purpose is linked with a simultaneous awareness
of both our powerlessness and aloneness *and* our intimate
connection with the ten thousand things, the experience of
nonself. I see these dual realizations as inseparable. That said,
there's no need to dwell on our isolation and separateness. Most
of us feel our separateness acutely, whether we're fully aware of
the reason for our pain or not. What we need is a way to connect,
to shed the blocks and destructive habits that are holding us
back. We need a way to generate hope. To unlock.

Still, the tribulations are part of the triumph. "No struggle, no
swag!" as I like to say. I came up with that slogan when I was
working with a women's Division II volleyball team at a college
in Southern California. I got the job through the coach, a friend
I had worked with when she was on staff at Boston College.

These girls were young, eighteen to twenty years old. I'm not
sure why, but it soon became apparent that they didn't want to
practice very hard. They didn't want to put in the time or make
the effort. They wanted a softer, easier way. They kept making
a fuss about all the training, both mental and physical, that
I put them through. "You got to be willing to work for it," I
told them. "You could be chillin' but you got to be willing. No
struggle, no swag!"

Chillin' and willing! No struggle, no swag! Sometimes I go hip-
hop, depending on my mood and the group that I'm riffing to.
Just letting it flow. Not being bound by convention or anything
else. There is a marked resonance, as though one has entered the
natural order of things.

No struggle, no swag. That could be a motto for everything we do in life. Without struggle, we don't grow. Without something to push against, we don't become stronger. It's not just a matter of physical strength either. It's the same for emotional resilience and wisdom. Nothing is worth anything if it's easy and effortless. It doesn't mean anything if you don't pay for it in sweat and blood (literal or metaphorical).

You got swag without struggle? That's not real swag. You can vividly see this in sports training, in an easily measurable way. That's one of the reasons why sport is such a potent metaphor and model for all kinds of other activities.

When we're struggling to find our authentic self, it's generally not going to happen without suffering. Uncovering the masterpiece within means facing our existential aloneness, the suffering that is the root of life. This is the first Noble Truth in Buddhism, and it is the insight of existentialism. We need to admit our feelings of loneliness and our related fears. To really *feel* them. With the admission of those feelings and fears comes the ability to be *vulnerable*, to admit that we often don't know what we're doing. Without vulnerability, how can we possibly be authentic?

I admit that I'm vulnerable. I don't have all the answers. But also that I am always investigating. I am completely committed to learning. I'm being mindful day by day, moment by moment. I'm walking, just walking. Putting one foot in front of the other. I'm going to figure it out. I may not be there yet, but I am sincere and absolutely committed.

You won't hear me saying, "I have the answer" or "Follow me." I'm not into that stuff. I'm saying, "See for yourself." The idea is for you to have a direct experience of the teaching. Find your true self, your own masterpiece. I want to help, and I will in whatever way I can. But ultimately, only you know what's right for you. You have to do it for yourself. I want you to be you. We all *need* you to be you. Your masterpiece is your offering to the world. We all need it, and we need you. We need everyone, every single person. We need all those masterpieces. Every one. I know this for a fact—not even one of us can be left behind.

NOW THAT WE HAVE TRAVELED SOME DISTANCE TOGETHER, I AM hopeful that you understand some of the mechanics of this journey to unlock your innate gifts, chip away the outer layers, with careful attention to body and mind. I hope you have discovered the joy of the success that comes from unleashing your authentic self. It starts with understanding that you are wholly unique and possess rare abilities, and it requires a willing descent into your past to wrestle with what stands in your way. We have to see where we're hiding out. And, you know, we have to recognize that we need help, that it's impossible to unlock on our own. Only with this kind of honesty and willingness and vulnerability do we emerge and begin to see a new path, a promise for what we can offer the world.

The goal may be in sight now, but there is still work to be done. We have already touched on the ways that changing your attitude and the way you see and respond to the world can change your life. Now let's delve deeper into understanding what that mental game is all about.

FREEDOM IS A STATE OF MIND

———

The function of freedom is to free someone else.

—Toni Morrison

Discovering freedom involves finding inner strength, perhaps a kind of fortitude and individuality and courage that we didn't even know we had. Often, it requires untethering ourselves from that which doesn't serve us. As we come into touch with the masterpiece within, we feel more ourselves; we gain new levels of awareness of what true freedom means for us.

A concrete example of this was Kobe's jump shot. He developed that shot by listening to his internal wisdom. He allowed what was inside him to speak for itself. He focused on what felt natural and right rather than on the many external voices and circumstances pushing for a more traditional approach: more arc, a different way to hold the ball. He rejected others' opinions, knowing that only he could find what was true and right for him. That's freedom. As the great novelist and poet Hermann Hesse said: "I live in my dreams—that's what you sense. Other people live in dreams, but not their own. That's the difference." We all need to stop living other people's dreams. We are all on our own unique path. In one sense, freedom is being able to see that and live it.

We tend to assume that our "inside" is colored by what's happening to us; that our internal state is largely determined by external circumstances. We do much better as human beings, however, when we flip that equation. Once you get your mind right, everything else falls into place. As bestselling author and self-help expert Wayne Dyer said: "If you change the way you look at things, the things you look at change."

Never was this more graphically illustrated for me than when I worked in prisons. Relatively early on in my recovery, I went into jails, hospitals, and substance abuse recovery centers as part of the Hospital and Institution Committee within Narcotics Anonymous and Alcoholic Anonymous. Recovering addicts would go in as a group and have a Twelve Step meeting in the place, and members of the group would share their experiences, strength, and hope. This was known as taking on a "service commitment."

When I first started working with inmates, I taught what we called "recovery-based training." We had programs about how to respond to a triggering event, such as running into someone you used to get high with; how to safely be around others who are drinking at a social event; and how to seek employment opportunities with integrity, being honest about your past and clearly stating your future aspirations.

My interest in helping people disadvantaged in one way or another continued through the 1980s. In late 1990, when I was living at the Cambridge Insight Meditation Center, I learned that a government agency had put forth a request for proposals (RFP) for someone to teach meditation and yoga to inmates. I eagerly wrote the proposal with guidance from Jon Kabat-Zinn, a friend and mentor. We both saw this opening as a calling, an opportunity to serve, and were delighted when I was awarded the contract.

This whole period in my life was about realizing that I needed to give back and share my transformation with others. Part of my underlying insight was that learning meant teaching and that my sobriety depended on giving my time and energy to people who needed me. I was doing what was in front of me. The next step always seemed to arrive just in time. After my initial hesitation when Larry suggested that I teach, I had shifted. My new attitude was that I was excited to teach anywhere to anyone. That was Larry's doing. He taught me to teach when asked to teach; if no one showed up, I was to teach anyway. I was living in the moment. I didn't reflect on what it meant; I was simply grateful for the opportunity.

Later, when I was tapped by legendary coach Phil Jackson and became part of the six NBA championship teams in a period of seven years—1996, 1997, 1998 with the Chicago Bulls, and 2000, 2001, and 2002 with the LA Lakers—that work felt like a natural extension of the teaching I had been doing at the CIMC and in prisons, as well as other counseling work I had done. The transition into the NBA felt natural at the time. Reflecting now on my experience, I wonder: How, really, did it happen? One day I was teaching inmates meditation and yoga, and the next I was sitting behind the Chicago Bulls' bench as the team made a run to the championship and coaching the greatest player in the game. In retrospect, it seems like a miracle. But at the time I was focused on the moment, keeping my life moving forward, doing what I knew how to do. The next step was something given. At the time, I really didn't know by whom or by what. But I knew to trust in the movement of life and to be grateful.

DOING TIME

When teaching inside the prison system, I wanted to alleviate suffering and help people tap into their potential. Helping these individuals at their lowest point was a challenge. Nearly all the inmates had trouble seeing their value, their potential gifts. They had been devalued by the system, pushed into thinking that they were somehow less than the rest of us.

The struggle to reach them, to connect, was hard, but it was nothing compared to the battle of facing what they faced. I taught skills that I knew helped them go inside their mind and discover the truth of who they were and who they could be. I wanted them to discover that they too had a masterpiece within. That they too could unlock. "Just remember—it's an inside job," I said, and we all had a laugh.

It's up to each one of us to access that masterpiece, to develop our own equivalent of Kobe's jump shot. It doesn't matter if you're serving life or living large—it's your interior mental state and ability to believe in what is right for you, and exercise it, that is ultimately what counts. You might think that yoga and meditation are hobbies for those living cushy lives. They often are, for sure—but the reality is that these tools are also lifesaving for those incarcerated. To be able to access and control your mind and body when other freedoms have been removed is a true and precious gift.

The Prison Project (the program for which we'd received the federal grant) ran for five years and taught me a tremendous amount. When I started, I wasn't expecting that—I thought I was there to help; I didn't know that I was also there to learn. Some of the inmates I worked with in prison had attained profound wisdom, and they became my teachers.

We worked in five prisons in eastern Massachusetts, including the Massachusetts Correctional Institution at Norfolk, Malcolm X's home away from home. By all accounts, Malcolm felt that prison was central to his development. He read voraciously while in prison, and converted to Islam. He found himself, developing his intellect. He used prison as his own personal retreat, if you will. That might seem a stretch to some folks. Yet after spending quite a bit of time in prisons working with inmates, I can see that that approach to doing time is not so far-fetched. In fact, some inmates use prison as a means to liberate themselves even as they're behind bars, even when they know they're not getting out—ever.

Some of the guys I taught were "double lifers," meaning that they were serving two consecutive life sentences, mostly for multiple murders; some had also been convicted of crimes such as assault and rape. These were a tough bunch, many of them well versed in the darker aspects of human nature. I wasn't a total stranger to this world: I had actually grown up with some of them, and they knew me from the old days as a drug fiend whose sole purpose in life was to get high. I knew them from the streets and from the shooting galleries and crack houses I had frequented. Imagine their surprise when I showed up in my little Chinese outfit, the kind David Carradine wore in the 1970s television series *Kung Fu*, which had made a big impression on me.

There's a saying in prison: You can do the time or let the time do you. I saw evidence of that over my years working in prisons. One of the things the prisoners with whom I worked taught me is that prison is a state of mind. As is freedom.

The double lifers were never getting out. And yet some of them were my best and most appreciative students. They would thank me for just being there. It struck them as miraculous that I would *voluntarily* enter their world. Or be interested in them. As mentioned, prison is a place where it's hard to feel your worth as a human being, to feel that you have any value. Inmates feel as though they've been "put away." Stashed in a forgotten place. They are "inside"; that's their reality. As a result, they're in a state of suspended animation. It's a very odd, difficult position.

Prisoners who were serving life sentences or even consecutive life sentences were not in denial about being there, despite the brutal reality of prison life. I knew guys who'd been in there for ten years, and they still didn't really believe it. We must consent to something being true in order to accept it as true. These prisoners acted as if they weren't in prison; they didn't take it seriously. They were not present; they were in denial. I know the feeling: I was in denial about my substance abuse until I admitted it and took responsibility for it.

In prison, when you take responsibility for your life, you do the time. You say, Yes, I'm in prison and I need to use my time wisely instead of acting as though nothing mattered.

The truth is that many of us have a tendency to live without taking responsibility for our actions and choices. We passively move from day to day, interaction to interaction, blaming others and the world for the things that make us unhappy. We see ourselves as acted upon rather than acting. We just go along with whatever is happening, detached and drifting. We don't fully embrace our connection to each other, opting instead to live selfishly. We live in a dream of our own making, and we shirk reaching out to help others, seeing that as too much effort and preferring to take care of ourselves.

Fortunately, for some inmates serving consecutive life sentences, the realization kicks in that yes, prison is where they are and where they're going to stay until they take their last breath. And they also realize that how they use the time inside will determine their quality of life. It's as the great African American novelist James Baldwin said: "Freedom is not something that anybody can be given; freedom is something people take and people are as free as they want to be." Another great African American novelist, Toni Morrison (quoted at the top of this chapter), said:

"Freeing yourself was one thing, claiming ownership of that freed self was another."

On one level we're all in the prison of our conditioning—that is, the ways we automatically react to what's happening around us and the self-image we've constructed and cling to tenaciously (though it bears little or no relationship to who we really are). We can either live trapped in that fantasy or wake up to the reality that we possess innate greatness and are capable of the unimaginable. And yet we are also existentially alone and helpless; that too is reality. Life feels infinitely precious and can be snuffed out at any second. Love and loss are inextricably linked. These paradoxes are at the heart of the human condition. They are also at the crux of my life as an addict and meditator, teacher and seeker.

The goal of bringing meditation and yoga to inmates through the Prison Project was to help them come back into their body, to be in the moment. You can imagine how hard it is in prison to actually be here now. It is natural to want to be elsewhere, to lose oneself in fantasies about the past or the future. To want to be anyplace else but behind bars. To be here now can shatter a person's psyche.

Many of the men I came to know were drowning in shame. Part of my job was to let them breathe again by helping them touch their innate wisdom. I also tried to give them a sense that greatness existed inside them too. Some of them thought that perhaps they might have possessed that greatness at some point—they could go that far—but most believed that it had been irrevocably extinguished by the choices they had made. And now most choices were being made *for* them.

It doesn't matter whether you're on the court in the NBA finals or in the prison where Malcolm X did time. The process—and the potential—is identical. No matter what you may have done, the greatness within is always present. Whether you're driving to the hoop for the game-winning shot or waiting in the lunch line in a windowless cafeteria for orange Jell-O—if you're free in your mind, you're free. Freedom is a state of mind. Liberation is something internal; it's a mental condition.

During my prison visits, that lesson applied to me as well as the inmates. The rooms the prison administration gave me to teach in were often funky—junk-filled storage spaces with low ceilings, concrete walls, and buzzing fluorescent lights. I had to mop the floor, wipe down the surfaces, make a functional space to hold class. This was not the serene, pristine, carpeted meditation hall with Buddha statues of the Cambridge Insight Meditation Center. The rooms they gave me were in no way conducive to what I was trying to teach: coming into the here and now; being in the moment; relaxation.

Buddhist monk and author Thich Nhat Hanh said: "Every breath we take, every step we make, can be filled with peace, joy, and serenity." To attain that state of mind is no easy task anywhere, and being inside Norfolk only made it harder. The prison atmosphere was stifling—a creeping, grinding sense of time battered into submission, time crawling on its hands and knees, barely able to inch forward. There was an airless

claustrophobia, a crypt-like staleness; the smell of ammonia
and boiled food; the body odor of men locked together in close
quarters, crushed against each other, breathing each other's air.
Boredom and oppression dulled the mind, and the place was
heavy with pain.

I often had long waits inside the facility to move from one area to
another; and not infrequently the whole place would be locked
down, and then I'd be stuck, locked in a windowless room. I had
to go through my own struggles during all that. Figuring out how
to be with it. The waiting. The mopping. The way the COs made
everything hard, throwing up obstacles to what I was trying to
do. They had no interest and saw no value in it. They resented
it and me, as though the people they lorded it over should not
be afforded any help, anything extra. As though the inmates'
existence should be as spartan and as bare of joy as possible.
The prisoners were being punished, after all. Rehabilitation?
The word comes from the Latin *habilitas*, to make able again, a
restoration of position or privilege. Most of the COs were deeply
cynical: they couldn't have cared less.

I had to change my own mind to cope with the surroundings
and the attitudes. It was a choice. I could grit my teeth and
accept the filthy room they gave me, the pointless periods of
waiting, the staff's disinterest or even hostility; I could give in
to the involuntary anger that rose inside me at the way some of
the COs saw the inmates as a subhuman species, to be treated
with contempt or even cruelty. Or I could take all that the job
entailed as an opportunity. To not react. To just do. To keep
generating hope and see it as service.

Kabat-Zinn writes about the idea of service in his book *Wherever You Go, There You Are*: "The only way you can do anything of value is to have the effort come out of non-doing and to let go of caring whether it will be of use or not. Otherwise, self-involvement and greediness can sneak in and distort your relationship to the work."

The non-doing I practiced involved responding without judgment or internal commentary to the task at hand. We can all cultivate that attitude. To just do by non-doing. To handle what's in front of us. Attend to it. One thing is like another. The feelings that arise from what are perceived as unpleasant situations or tasks are just that—feelings. They come and go. They are internal weather. Why attach to them? Do what needs doing. Wait. Mop. It doesn't matter. Do your time. Don't let the time do you.

The first thing I taught the inmates (and it was something I practiced myself) was how to stop being reactive; to slow down, remain calm, rest, and heal. I realized that slow was smooth and smooth is fast, as I would come to teach athletes. When it's smooth, you're not tripping over yourself, getting caught up, wasting time and energy.

I developed an exercise for helping inmates slow down. In those windowless rooms, under the buzzing florescent lights, I had my students keep their breathing slow and deep and steady.

Here's the exercise that I had them do. Please try this wherever you are:

Visualize a pristine mountain lake. The lake is very quiet and still. The water, unruffled, reflects high, untouched, snowcapped peaks all around, and cloudless sky. Forests of deep evergreen border the water. Let this image rest in your mind as you keep your breathing deep and slow.

Then imagine dropping a stone into the middle of the lake. Imagine it slowly sinking down and down through the cool, clean water. Let it sink slowly in time with the rhythm of your breath. Imagine it sinking to the bottom of the lake, where it gently settles. Let yourself rest with that stone in the cool, clean depths.

The goal of this exercise is to move us from fight, flight, and freeze mode to rest and digest. Our nervous system is typically calibrated so that our left brain—the rational, reasoning, planning, active, directed part of us—is dominant. Our left brain knows absolutely nothing about non-doing (at least for a right-handed person). It takes credit for everything. In other words, we think that anything of any worth is a result of *our* doing. We are self-centered and self-important: our underlying assumption is that the whole of human accomplishment rests in our hands. We're in a rush and impatient. Why waste any more time? Let's get to it, fix it up, and solve the world's problems. And no one had better get in our way.

We can see that with this attitude it's quite difficult for anything truly new to emerge. We are mostly tinkering with and perhaps extending coordinates that have already been established. We would do well to remember what Yoda said to Luke Skywalker: "You must unlearn what you have learned."

That's all well and good, the planning, active, rational part of us says. But one plus one always equals two. We can build on that.

Is that true, though? Does one plus one always equal two? Is there not a reality beyond what we can see? Are there not things we have felt that yet are unseen? How does the *new* come into being?

Perhaps, we might say, the new comes into being from something extra that we can't necessarily identify because we haven't discovered it yet. One day, perhaps, when our science is more advanced, we'll know what that extra something is and be able to quantify it. It's hard to imagine a time far in the future when we'll have it *all* figured out. In any case, that's a hypothetical. In the here and now, from one perspective, we as a species have come a long way from the darkness of our caves, and we know a lot. But on the other hand, we still have a lot to learn.

I take that as a good thing. That not-knowing allows the new to emerge. The unknown. The unexpected. The surprising. That's what makes life interesting. We can help create conditions for the new to happen. When we focus on meditation or prayer, the left brain stops being so dominant and then the right brain—with our intuitive, creative, imaginative capacities—comes into play. I often had the inmates sit and breathe and be with what I call the "awareness of breathing." I invited them to be with the breath. To keep returning their awareness to the breath. To be aware of the duration and speed of the breath. Of breathing in and breathing out. To feel the breath moving into and out of the body. To feel the breath in the whole body, from head to toes, entering and leaving. I encourage you to try this as well.

We could spend a lifetime on just this one practice.

By keeping our awareness on the breath, we can slow things down. The tempo of experience shifts. With that comes control, and the ability to respond rather than react. It's the same thing I would go on to teach Kobe and MJ: how to cultivate and become intimate with the interior terrain between stimulus and response, between input and output, between what you feel and how you act. In basketball, when you're able to do that, players say the game "slows down." You can actually see that happen sometimes. Something shifts and suddenly a player will be "in rhythm." The game suddenly feels easy. There's syncopation. When players are in this mode, they often say something like: "I'm letting the game come to me." It's about responding rather than reacting, as I just said. To react is to be on automatic, as involuntary as an echo. To respond, on the other hand, is to come into tune with, to resonate and align with. That distinction holds true on the basketball court or behind bars.

The practice of opening up, expanding, and inhabiting that interior space was what allowed the inmates to feel that even though they were in prison, they were in control of their life. They had flipped the equation. Their inside was determining their outside. They were doing time rather than letting time do them. Some of those double lifers were freer than most people walking the streets. They were at peace with themselves. I could talk about the Buddha, Jesus, or Muhammad—it didn't matter. They were truly open, able to move in any direction inwardly, as though the constriction in their freedom of movement on the outside had led to the development of inner mobility, perhaps much the way someone who loses their sight will develop an incredibly acute sense of hearing. These prisoners, in touch with the vastness of their interior, were mental travelers who were free to roam. They had surrendered to life exactly as it was and had an unshakable equanimity. Nothing could move them off their sense of inner peace. They treated the prison like a monastery and their cage like a monk's cell.

This is liberation of the mind. Liberation means that even in the most horrendous circumstances we know we have a choice about how we respond to what's happening around us. Even in Dachau or Auschwitz. Even in a Siberian gulag. We always have a choice in how we respond. To know that and to act in light of that knowledge in all circumstances and conditions—that, to me, is the definition of freedom.

BEING ATTUNED TO THE UNDERWORLD

My street smarts from growing up in the hood helped me during my prison work. The classes I taught were closely monitored; only those people who had been cleared and had registered were allowed in. It was crucial that the inmates felt safe enough to relax, to close their eyes, focus on their breathing, and quiet their minds. That meant no strangers and no surprises.

A few years into this teaching regimen, I was in my regular spot and noticed a new guy come into the room. He was built like a bull. His big head was set on a short neck that looked as thick around as a tree trunk, and he had a wedge of curly black hair. His shoulders and hips were almost as wide as the door. There was a vibe about him. I won't say it was evil, but it was very, very negative. I could feel the energy moving through him. I was up out of my chair in a second and with two steps went smoothly to meet him—nothing jarring or untoward, just moving toward him in a state of relaxed alertness. When we feel a threat, this is often the most helpful posture to assume. We need to meet the energy that's coming at us, but we don't want to accelerate it or amplify it. We need to use a gentle kind of power. Unlocking means being centered in yourself. In the same way that we're able to retain an inner equanimity regardless of outward circumstances, we can retain a calm and gentle—yet firm—force in the face of anger or people who for whatever reason are acting out or intend to do us harm.

So . . . I approached him. His head was sunk into his thick neck, his eyes hooded under his dark brow. I occupied a space near him that was not too close, but close enough to make my presence felt without tripping what I could sense was his hair trigger. A person learns to gauge this distance, a very nuanced and precise proximity, on the streets in the neighborhoods where I grew up.

I kept my breathing deep and regular, maintaining an internal space and a vibration that was both relaxed and alert. We know this "poised" state when we see it in sports. Watching football, basketball, or baseball, we see it when players stand in a way that lets you know they're awake, alert, and ready to act.

One thing about cats in prison, many of whom grew up in violent neighborhoods, as I did: our instincts are honed. We learn to read the street and read people. We become acutely attuned to an underworld, the life below the surface of life. This instinctual awareness is an assessing and feeling intelligence that's based in the body and that processes subtle sensations and subliminal signals. It senses fear and is attuned to danger. It is also prescient, seeing in advance how things are going to go down. You know in those movies where the hero sees exactly how each move in the fight is going to happen before the fight even begins? It's kind of like that, but not so hokey.

After I got clean, I was amazed—I'd be walking down the street with my girlfriend, who had grown up in the suburbs; she had no idea what was going down on the corners and in dark doorways and in the tight little cuts between the triple-deckers. She didn't notice the hooded watchfulness of the dealers; the distinctively jittery, cantered gait of the junkies looking to score; guys in cars cruising by, scoping the scene, maybe looking for someone to hurt. Few families were untouched by violence in the neighborhoods in which I grew up. My cousin, for example, was caught by a stray bullet in a drive-by shooting. He was on his bicycle, just riding around, a lovely kid; his mother, my aunt, was crushed by grief.

From that first encounter with the new guy in my prison group, I was able to establish a dynamic that made it clear that I was not to be messed with—and perhaps more important, that this *space* was not to be messed with. He turned and left without any overt confrontation. When we're centered inside ourselves, when we're unlocked, we can often diffuse difficult situations in just that way. What escalates conflicts is often meeting force with a similar type of volatility. If we can remain calm and centered and take the hostility directed at us and reflect it back as a clear, unruffled presence, that will often be enough to diffuse a difficult situation.

You can try this yourself. When you feel anger coming to the surface in response to something or someone, come back to your breath. Focus on keeping it moving in and out of your nostrils, throat, and abdomen. Resist the temptation to meet force with force. This does not mean to turn the other cheek. It means to breathe and to retain a position of inquiry and a detached but firm openness.

I learned later that my instincts had been right—this bull-necked man was in prison for murder. He looked strangely familiar, but I had forgotten the details. Turns out that I had been a juror on his first murder trial, which ended in a mistrial. He did, indeed, mean me harm. I dealt with him by absorbing his energy and sending it back at him in a gentle yet forceful way, and he chilled out.

My time in the prisons, and particularly this encounter, made me appreciate the ways in which my tough upbringing had given me a keen intuitive appreciation of where the boundaries are, in regard to acting in a way that escalates or defuses a situation that's in danger of getting out of hand.

Learning this awareness isn't limited to those who come from tough backgrounds. The body has its own intuitive intelligence. In the same way that I learned how to listen to my body when it was telling me that I was stressed or overwhelmed, I came to learn in my teaching that we can get quick and accurate reads on what other people are thinking and feeling. And further, if we can register their intensity and absorb its impact without flinching or throwing up walls or doing the equivalent of counterpunching—if, in other words, we respond to their intensity with calm firmness, which we could also call relaxed alertness—we can often gain control of the situation, no matter how explosive it initially seemed. This is true in the heat of the fourth quarter in a tight NBA game or during a tense negotiation in the corporate world. It's all about coming from the intelligence of the body, listening to the body, acting from the place of intuitive awareness, and letting *that* lead instead of our preconceptions, which can often spur us to become hard and brittle and create the explosion that comes when force meets force.

USING GENTLE FORCE

I learned gentle force in its essential form by studying the martial arts. They're all about working with intuitive awareness, and they were a crucial piece of my inner development when I was working in the prisons. The prisons and the dojo, the space where martial arts are taught, complemented each other. They were both about deepening my trust in the intuitive aspects of myself. The dojo showed me to not denigrate or dismiss the intuitive aspects of myself as part of my former scuffling life, but rather to see if those qualities that were strong inside me could be used and developed and trusted. I was particularly drawn to tai chi, because it emphasizes the subtle nuances of power and force in ways that are especially sophisticated and refined. I saw that tai chi was uniquely suited for teaching in prisons. If you want to gain control and command respect in a prison classroom, you need to set firm boundaries up front without being aggressive. Then, after you've established those boundaries, you can back off a bit and loosen up. But if the boundaries aren't there from the jump, and if they aren't firm, you can quickly get into trouble.

I learned the use of gentle force from Bow Sim Mark, a diminutive woman from China who moved to the US and set up a dojo in Boston's Chinatown. She was a grand master in many different forms of martial arts, but you probably haven't heard of her unless you're a martial artist. You may have heard of her son Donnie Yen, though; he's a tremendously successful actor and director of martial arts films based in Hong Kong, perhaps best known for the IP Man series.

Bow Sim Mark taught the combined style of tai chi. Her dojo was called the Chinese Wushu Research Institute. I found out about it when I was living at the Cambridge Insight Meditation Center through one of my meditation brothers. I was already studying tai chi, but I felt as though I needed another teacher. I went to Bow Sim Mark's classes and immediately felt as though I found my sifu, the Chinese honorific for teacher or master. I did group classes with Bow Sim Mark, and I also had private lessons with her.

Tai chi suited me. I viewed it as a fluid, graceful exercise rather than the practice of a martial art. A Black guy punching and kicking and shouting or, worse, wielding a sword in public tends to make people uptight and can lead to unpredictable results for the Black man in question—in this case, me. That was not the case with the slow, seemingly placid movements of tai chi. White people loved it. Look at the cool Black dude floating on air. Is he dancing? I could practice tai chi anywhere without anyone getting nervous.

Sifu called me Georgie. Although small—just five feet in her flat-soled, black canvas tai chi slippers—she was powerful beyond reckoning. She could move me around effortlessly, even though I was much bigger and physically stronger. In the way I learned to do with angry inmates, she would use my own energy against me, throwing me off balance and redirecting me with ease.

You could feel her strength and power in the way she moved. And yet you were also aware of a tremendous gentleness, a calm fluidity, flexibility, and grace that came from a life devoted to circular, flowing movement and the balancing of yin and yang, which may appear opposite—masculine-feminine, hard-soft, heaven-earth—but are really complementary. Tai chi exercises are said to improve and support health by moving energy through the body's channels. Tai chi is known as a "soft" form or an "internal" martial art. Although its relationship to actual combat can seem far removed, that is an illusion. It could be thought of as the most refined fighting form, medicinal exercise, moving meditation, or dance. Or all of these at once.

In the exercise class we did on Mondays, there was a lot of stretching and we had to do full splits, where I strained with all my might to get my ass to the floor. Bow Sim Mark watched me, much amused at my antics. "Georgie, Georgie," she said. "Can you afford it?" I think what she meant was "Can you handle it?" But I was never quite sure. These splits were excruciating. My tight tendons, my groin, and the underside of my legs felt as though they were being filleted.

When one of her students passed away, Sifu asked me to drive her to the service. It felt like an honor to spend quality time alone with her. She hadn't seen the student who had died in years, and yet her commitment to him was still strong enough to take the time and make the trip. When you have a teacher like that and she asks you to do something, you do it—no questions asked.

Tai chi now informs everything I do. I meet hard with soft; I absorb and transmute and send force coming at me back in a way that relies on the basic form I learned. My movements are circular and flowing. I work with the graceful arcs of the tai chi form to help people take their aggression and negativity and difficulties and turn them into something beautiful and true. By making the hard soft, we transform so many of life's difficulties. What seems aggressive and intractable, a threatening assault that contorts us into an uncomfortable position or painfully pushes and pokes, becomes harmless. Being unlocked gives this kind of equanimity and poise, openness and curiosity. We have room for more of life, even if that "more" is not so pleasant. *Every* aspect of life is worthy of our attention and consideration.

Tai chi ran a parallel course and resonated with what I was learning at the Cambridge Insight Meditation Center about the breath: that the whole universe is contained within it. This was also the case with each and every movement within the tai chi form, as well as the form itself.

"Your whole life, Georgie," Sifu would say, teaching me. Meaning you can spend your whole life just working with this one small thing—maybe the way your pelvis turns as your arm goes out. Her perspective gave me an appreciation for the most seemingly minute forms of physical posture and movement—a millimeter can make all the difference in the world. This is where great athletes live, in those subtle shadings and minute adjustments. As we unlock, we become sensitive to the way the slightest things can make all the difference. The way we wash the dishes is not separate from how we treat each other. *All* of life demands of us care, attention, and appreciation. *Every* human being is worthy of respect.

"Your whole life, Georgie. Your whole life."

Sifu called her place a research institute, as I mentioned. That's because it was about discovery. She was a grand master of the highest rank, but she was still investigating, still finding out and digging deeper. There was no bottom to it. No end. Her goal was understanding—to really think about and investigate what she was doing. And she encouraged us to make discovery our goal too. There was something glorious about this quest, and a bit maddening: to give yourself over to seeking rather than finding. It was so open-ended. There was always more. And you knew you would never master even a fraction of it. Sifu asked us to cultivate a spirit of inquiry, an exquisite inquisitiveness and commitment to embrace the unknown. And to do it with joy. That was the spirit of her dojo, and I carry that spirit with me in everything I do. We can all adopt that mindset even if we don't study tai chi or meditate. It comes when we discover that essence inside us that connects to the rest of life and is inseparable from it. That's the mental game: coming back again and again to this realization, even when that's hard to do. No struggle, no swag.

The dojo was a simple space on the ground floor. Nothing fancy. Chinatown was a tough part of town. People hung around the Chinatown area to do drugs, and there was prostitution. Sifu didn't seem to notice. She eventually moved to West Newton. That was at the end of my studies with her. Later, though, she returned to Chinatown. When I was traveling all the time, working with the Bulls and Lakers, it was hard for me to keep learning from her. Her forms involved a steadiness and regular times for practice. Working with a teacher like that involves constancy and commitment. The flow of my life was taking me elsewhere. But what she taught me remains alive and radiant and moving inside me to this day.

WHAT I LEARNED FROM SIFU HELPED STRENGTHEN MY UNDER-standing of firmness and power married to gentleness and compassion. She taught me that the internal translates into the external. If we are calm inside, we can pacify the aggression and hostility we encounter. We can take the negativity coming at us and transmute it into something neutral and harmless. This is freedom, to not be at the mercy of whatever is coming down the pike. And it doesn't matter if you're in an eight-by-ten-foot cell or a mansion in Beverly Hills—the process is the same. In one way, doing that essential work is easier in a cell, because there are fewer places to hide, fewer distractions. The mansion, if we're so disposed, has endless hideouts.

In both the prisons and the dojo, I learned that we need to trust our intuitive awareness, really respect that part of ourselves and give it its due. When we honor our interior in this way, we begin to experience a kind of vastness inside us that is ripe for exploration. We should not think that the masterpiece inside us is some small, discrete thing to be picked up and admired. It is vast and all-encompassing. Unlocking is not about one aspect of what we do and who we are. It is pervasive.

I learned from the prisoners that we really are free, regardless of circumstances—that it is really our responses that determine the quality of our lives, not what befalls us. Until we are able to elevate into that consciousness, we will have the feeling of being trapped on the surface of things in much the same way a bird beats itself on a pane of glass trying to escape into the open air that it can clearly see but can't access. Until we realize our divine essence, we will feel half-formed and shackled, locked up in a prison of our own making.

CONSCIOUS CONNECTION

———————

We need the courage to learn from our past and not live in it.

—Sharon Salzberg

The hard-soft of tai chi, the way it teaches us to use gentle force and to experience the body as fluid and flowing and in tune with the inner movement of life, helped me touch the masterpiece within, the part of me that was connected to what I'll call, for lack of better words, the divine, the sacred, God, Christ consciousness, a higher power, suchness, thusness, atman, the ground of being, our true self, the Buddha within, the true self, the authentic self, the divine essence, the source, and the greatness within. Don't be fooled by these names or think that because we have named this essence, we have found it! All these names point to an ultimately ungraspable mystery.

Still, whatever it is that we're seeking—that which we can feel but not necessarily see—is quite tangible and real. It is always present inside us. We have all experienced it. We have all had the feeling of being one with the flow of life. We have felt it when we are broken open by grief or agape, in awe or exultation. At those moments, we feel that we know, finally, what life is all about. The veil has been stripped away and we acutely feel the presence of something larger than ourselves. This, to put one of the above-listed names on it, is the higher power that is so crucial to AA and recovery.

Part of what attracted me to drugs was that, at first, altering my consciousness allowed me to leave my small self behind. Yes, I also got into drugs because I wanted to have fun. Nevertheless, early on drugs did give me a feeling that my consciousness was expanded, and I had a yearning for that type of insight and experience. I would learn, of course, that addiction is a dead end. Drugs can give you glimpses of that higher power. But they most often devolve into a narrow selfishness: your whole world is reduced to a single mantra: *I need to get high now*.

As I continued my recovery, pursued my prison work, went deeper into my meditation practice, and became a teacher of mindfulness, I began to see that I needed to change that selfish orientation. When we connect to a higher power, to the divine, we see that life is about helping others strengthen their conscious connection to the divine. And in order to do that, I knew that in my own life the task was to stay connected, in conscious contact with the greatness within. The question became how to sustain that connection.

Why is it we're often so lax with this connection? Isn't it the most important thing? Is it perhaps because what we're after is ungraspable? Once we think we've caught it, we've lost it. One of the deeper lessons of the flowing truth of tai chi is that everything is always changing, transforming, turning. It is not an *it*.

There were times early on when I felt so far from my true nature that it seemed unattainable, infinitely distant, forever beyond me. Sometimes we don't know where that true nature has gone until something happens—maybe something amazing, maybe something absolutely awful. Revered Buddhist teacher and author Pema Chodron writes beautifully about the realizations that happen when we're "broken open" by those inevitable events in life that are out of our control. Chodron, who comes out of the Tibetan Buddhist tradition, expresses a truth similar to one from the Hasidic branch of Judaism, which teaches that there is nothing as whole as a broken heart.

THERE IS AN AXIOM: WHEN THE STUDENT IS READY, THE TEACHER will appear. That's another way of saying, When you're ready for the experience, it will manifest. We all have lessons that the universe is telling us we need to learn. And if we don't learn a particular lesson, we will keep getting it until we do learn it. I like to say, What we resist persists. When I think about my own experience and my unfolding, it's the adversity I experienced that allowed the unfolding to happen.

No struggle, no swag! It's important to recognize that we need to be able to tolerate discomfort. We have to stretch ourselves in order to grow. That's how the brain works. Everything has got to be a struggle. It's got to be hard to do—but doable. We have to be able to get beyond our limits and push through. We must embrace challenges and the unpleasantness that comes from stretching ourselves in ways that are uncomfortable.

That stretching is one way we keep strengthening our conscious connection to the divine. Another part of the process is maintaining the awareness that everything is changing. So how we connect has to change. We can't just find one way and say, Eureka, I've found it! That's a recipe for disaster.

We need to bring ourselves back to what's fluid, changeable. We must be flexible in our approach. Spontaneous.

One of the ways I try to maintain conscious connection to the greatness within is by reading, praying, and meditating. These activities—and others—help me understand the nature of my own mind and the universe. Through reading, I've come to know that all spiritual traditions are pointing at the same truth: that there is an illusion of separateness and that the conscious connection to the divine that we all seek comes about through the experience of love.

We know this, of course, not just through reading but through our own experience. Love is what aligns us to divinity. In that alignment we find ourselves far from the experiences of greed, hatred, and delusion. The experience of love that I'm pointing toward here arises through generosity, compassion, and understanding. I keep this awareness of what generates love front and center.

I see my struggles and travails as a joyful journey of discovery. We can all do this. Maybe not always in the moment when life hurts, but always by directing ourselves in this direction, back to the mystery and the unnameable essence.

I've been on this journey for almost forty years. Forty years in recovery. Part of my ongoing recovery is that every morning I connect with the divine presence. Every morning I am reading and praying and meditating. Every morning I am working to strengthen my conscious connection. That is what teaching is about for me, expressing what is inside and letting it flow in whatever way it wants to go. The conscious connection I'm describing is not something that happens automatically. We have to work at it, and we can never take it for granted.

We could say the same thing about love. Too often, we think love is something that just happens. It is the result of Cupid's arrow, fired from the realm of gods. It is signaled by a thunderbolt, descending from above. Capriciously and mysteriously, it strikes or wells up within and overwhelms us. Then we possess it and are possessed by it and our whole is consumed by it. Is this really love? Is that what we're talking about when we talk about the masterpiece within or Christ consciousness or the sacred? Authentic love is not something transient. It is always there, always present, no matter how distant and impossible it sometimes seems. It simply needs to be revealed. Unlocked.

I don't want to say what love is. Love is many things. Love is like Joseph Campbell's *A Hero with a Thousand Faces*. Except its faces are infinite.

UNDIMINISHED ENTHUSIASM

My prayer practice helps keep me connected to divinity, to the masterpiece and greatness within. Prayer is a way to make the conscious connection we were just considering. One prayer that has worked for me right from the beginning of my recovery is the Serenity Prayer by American theologian Reinhold Niebuhr, which was adapted in a shortened form by Alcoholics Anonymous: "God grant me the serenity to accept the things I cannot change, courage to change the things I can, and wisdom to know the difference."

The eleventh step in the program has also been adapted into a prayer, which likewise is important to me, particularly its emphasis on *service*: "God, direct my thinking today so that it be empty of self-pity, dishonesty, self-will, self-seeking and fear. God, inspire my thinking, decisions and intuitions. Help me to relax and take it easy. Free me from doubt and indecision. Guide me through this day and show me my next step. God, show me what I need to do to take care of any problems. I ask all these things that I may be of maximum service to you and my fellow man. In the spirit of the Steps I pray. Amen."

This prayer is about improving our conscious contact with the greatness that exists in all of us. The greatness within is active. It is both being and becoming. We seek to attune to and resonate with its emergent energy. We seek the knowledge of divine will and the power to carry that out. Prayer is not about "Give me this or give me that." It is about "Thy will be done." The restoration of the kingdom. We pray for knowledge and the power to carry that out. For me, prayer and meditation overlap, but meditation is really about attunement, just letting the spirit flow through me. Prayer has more to do with asking myself to come into alignment with divine will.

What did Jesus Christ teach? Really only two things: love everybody and practice continual forgiveness. That is what I practice; that is what I pray to have the strength and wisdom to do.

When I pray, I elevate my mind. I'm thinking about love and divinity. I'm thinking about community, and I'm thinking about service. I'm thinking about the best version of myself and getting in touch with the divine inside me, seeking to feel that presence and to see it in others. In everyone really, without exception. I pray for the spirit to move inside me. There's a conscious return to innocence during prayer, a sincerity and naïveté. We need to shed the attitude that we're too cool for innocence. It was Jesus who said we should become like children again to enter the kingdom of heaven.

THE REASON I THINK ABOUT COMMUNITY DURING PRAYER IS that I believe our lives are shaped by the relationships we engage in, and that we come to know ourselves by how we relate to others. We live in networks of connections and intimacy. We can have a direct experience of our deep affinity with each other— and when we sense that affinity, it moves us beyond the illusion of separateness.

"Teamwork makes the dream work." "It's better together." These are little sayings that I keep in mind and use when I'm team building in sports and other venues, such as schools, institutions, or businesses. We need to remember that we are social creatures. We help others and by doing so we help ourselves.

Twelve Step recovery groups are a great example of this. The community of AA has helped millions of people overcome their addictions to food, drugs, alcohol, gambling, sex, and other substances and behaviors. The Twelve Step fellowship is a powerful, supportive community. One of the tenets that make it work is its emphasis on helping other people free themselves from their addictions. I certainly came to realize that the best way to help myself is to forget myself and help others help themselves. I stay loving and peaceful by helping others do the same. I want to keep being loving and peaceful, and the way to do that is to give those attitudes away to others. We can all practice this: teaching love and peace is the best way to learn about love and peace. This path to the masterpiece within is available to all of us, in all our relationships and interactions.

TO MAKE A CONSCIOUS CONNECTION WITH THE GREATNESS within, we have to cultivate an openness and a willingness to allow love to move in us and through us. The more open we are, the more love is going to express itself through us. Love is not coming from out there to in here. It's already inside us. How much can we get out of our own way and allow it to flow? That is the challenge.

We all have the ability. Are we willing to get in touch with it? Sometimes that connection just happens and we're suddenly conscious of it. Think of the adage, A broken clock tells the right time twice a day. It's the same with our awareness of our connection to something larger than ourselves. Once in a while we get it. The spirit moves us. We're not doing anything special— and there it is. How did it happen?

Perhaps we could think of it as the law of averages. In many games, Babe Ruth struck out in his first two times at bat. After those strikeouts, he'd often walk back to the dugout smiling. The third time up he might have two strikes against him and then just belt a pitch, sending it out of the ballpark. He'd jog around the bases and return to the dugout with the same smile he'd had when he'd gone down swinging.

Sometimes, when he struck out, even the great Babe Ruth was booed by the fans. When he wasn't hitting, the fans taunted him. And when he belted one, they exploded with joy. He kept smiling the same smile in either case because he knew that the law of averages was going to catch up with him. He knew his time would come, and he was going to connect with the ball and hit a doozy.

The Boston Red Sox couldn't handle the Babe. He was always carousing, and Boston was basically a small town in those days. Everybody was up in your face and knew your business. The Red Sox traded Ruth to the New York Yankees. New York was a different kind of place than Boston: it gave him the privacy he needed to indulge his wild ways.

The Babe embodied a spirit we can all emulate. He was a big, lovable guy, and he just kept smiling, regardless of circumstances. That's the spirit! Strikeout or home run, have faith that the law of averages is going to come around. The doldrums will end. The wind will pick up. Generate that hope.

You know the most amazing thing to me about the Babe? He was an orphan. Despite having lost his parents early on, he was still able to smile at life. That's a way to access the masterpiece within. Boos or cheers—we don't let the environment determine whether we're happy or not, whether we smile or not. It is what it is, we might say. And we try to embrace it, no matter what.

Ruth struck out 1,300 times, and he also hit 714 home runs. Each time his bat missed the ball he knew that eventually he'd send one sailing into the stands. And each time he went up to the plate, he went as if he was going to get after it. He was smiling and undaunted, no matter what had happened in previous at-bats. He took his stand in the batter's box and welcomed whatever came.

We can all have that attitude. Each time we go up to bat, we're going to get after it. Winston Churchill famously said that the definition of success is going from failure to failure with undiminished enthusiasm.

Strike out or crush one. No matter the outcome, keep generating hope. Approach life with undiminished enthusiasm. Be of service. Be willing to open yourself and let love flow. That is the attitude we can all adopt to help us unlock and strengthen our conscious connection to the greatness within.

FROM SHOOTING SMACK TO SHOOTING HOOPS

No matter how diligent and committed we are to cultivating conscious contact with our true nature, ultimately what being in the moment and letting the moment speak to us is about is getting out of our own way. When we train and when we compete at a high level in sports, business, or any other field, our work always involves getting the hell out of our own way and letting instinct take over.

All the top athletes with whom I've worked have known this. All the training and preparation and thought and planning only establish a platform, a foundation, for something else to happen. We establish conscious contact in the practices described above; but at the end of the day, spirit cannot be forced, love cannot be coerced or summoned at will. Formulas and force are anathema to the flow of spirit, to the flow of love.

This was one of the key lessons I needed to impart to the Chicago Bulls team of 1993–94. But I had no idea that that's what I would be teaching. When I joined the team as a personal and organizational development consultant, Phil Jackson and I had no idea how it was going to play out. The Bulls had already won three championships and were full of swag after dominating the league for so long, but they were also at a pivotal and fragile moment with Jordan gone.

It happened like all things did in my life after I got clean and sober and began to cultivate conscious contact with the masterpiece within. One thing led to another with a kind of inevitability, as though the stars had aligned in a certain way and life was unfolding in accord with a prearranged plan. Which is ironic, I suppose, given that what I was learning was to be spontaneous. To follow my instincts and intuitions and to listen to my heart.

I was doing my prison work through the University of Massachusetts Medical Center in Worcester, teaching mindfulness-based stress reduction and relaxation (MBSR). In graduate school, I had studied not only psychology but also group dynamics and organizational dynamic theory. My girlfriend at the time joked that I was a natural at group dynamics because I'd been born into a group of thirteen kids. She was right. I was able to transfer what I had learned innately, almost in spite of myself, in my family growing up to my work with programs in the Medical Center and then to professional sports teams (with their own unique, complex organizational structures) and also to business and educational organizations. The way they functioned, their various hierarchies, made intuitive sense to me. My corporate background also helped. In my earlier job as a senior financial analyst, I'd had to know what everyone in the company was doing and how much it cost, including what people made in salary and bonuses. I understood how my organization was structured, how the system worked from top to bottom. This background would come into play in my work with the Bulls.

Phil had coached the Bulls to three championships (1991–1993) before I came on board. They were a seemingly unstoppable force, largely due to the spectacular play of superstar Michael Jordan.

That July—after the 1993 championship but before the start
of the 1993–94 season—the unthinkable happened. Michael
Jordan's father, James Jordan, was murdered while sleeping in
his Lexus along a highway in North Carolina, apparently the
random victim of a robbery gone bad.

The news of the murder devastated Michael. He was extremely
close to his father, who had come to all of MJ's games and
traveled with the Bulls. When he learned of his father's death,
MJ announced his retirement from basketball, saying he had lost
his passion for the game. Without that passion he wasn't going
to be able to compete at the highest level, he said—and if he
couldn't do that, he just wasn't interested.

Phil was left with a team that had just won three championships
in a row but had lost their superstar. It was an unprecedented
situation, to say the least, and Phil was trying to figure out how
to move forward, to forge a new team identity and be successful
without the main piece of the team's former triumphs. He
knew the Bulls were in danger of imploding from the stress on
the players—stress that had been ratcheted up to an almost
unbearable level with MJ's sudden departure. Jordan had
defined the team and been their engine. He had focused the
eyes of the world on Chicago, and he had brought them to three
consecutive championships. Now what?

Phil had to coach the Bulls through what he called "the stress
of success." He knew how much pressure they were under,
though people on the outside couldn't see it. When you have
that kind of success, people are always coming at you. Your

relatives and friends want tickets. Strangers want a piece of you. You're constantly being asked to pay attention to someone else's needs. When you're winning, it's as if you had a target on your back. Everybody's gunning for you. Journalists want interviews. Companies are after you to promote their products; they want to give you things. You get a lot of attention, and that can take over and pull you out of the game and into something else. You can forget the work you need to do and become distracted. The mental and physical tolls impact the results, and your game suffers. Whatever level of conscious connection you've achieved is in jeopardy. You're pulled away from your internal knowing, and the noise of the outside world deafens you to your inner voice.

Phil wanted me to come in to help with the stress of success, but that was only part of it. His primary goal was helping his players continue to grow and evolve as whole people. You know, critics sometimes diss Phil and diminish his accomplishments. They say the only reason he won all those championships was because he had such great players. This is a ridiculous statement. Other coaches, such as Doug Collins and Mark Jackson, had great players on their teams who did not win championships but whose teams immediately following Collins's and Jackson's departures went on to win championships. It doesn't make these coaches bad. Talent is often the hardest thing to coach. Trust me and anyone else who works with incredibly talented individuals. One not only needs to bring out individual potential but to get the group clicking as a team. Phil had the remarkable capacity to do both.

Part of what made him successful as a promoter of teamwork was his background. Both his parents were ministers, and Phil treated his players as though they were his congregation. He was always thinking about them and praying for them. He did not see them as a means to an end. He saw them as developing and evolving people who needed to be treated as individuals. It was never one size fits all for Phil; he truly wanted his players, every one of them, to succeed both on and off the court.

With MJ gone, Phil knew he needed help, and he turned first to Jon Kabat-Zinn, who was teaching mindfulness and stress reduction at the Omega Institute that summer. Was there someone Jon knew whom his players would trust and relate to and who could bring them more deeply into the kinds of meditative techniques Phil had introduced them to but was really no expert in, and could that person also help them with the stress and the expectations they faced?

Phil's interest in meditation was already well known. His nickname around the NBA was Zen Master because of his spiritual approach to the game. In his book *Sacred Hoops: Spiritual Lessons of a Hardwood Warrior*, Phil writes about working to instill an awareness of the spiritual dimension of the game in his players, offering lessons that are applicable not only to basketball and sports but also to life. Phil taught his players meditation to help them clear their minds so they would be better able to act decisively and make split-second decisions without thinking. Meditation helped them to "just be" and to "just do" (the arrow shoots itself). Phil also taught his team a kind of samurai code, which involved respecting the

enemy (the opposing team and its players); it involved being
aggressive without being angry or violent. He stressed the
tribal aspect of team sports, an approach derived from his deep
involvement with Native American rituals and myths. (His
Lakota name, Wanbli Luzahan—given to him by the American
Indian College Fund as a sign of respect—means Swift Eagle.)
Phil's spiritual work with his players was enormously effective.
When he eventually retired from the Lakers, he had won eleven
championship rings (two as a player with the New York Knicks
and thirteen with the teams he'd coached).

When Phil asked Jon if he knew anyone who could help the
team with meditation and stress reduction, my name came
immediately to Jon's mind, given my background with the
game—particularly my association with Dr. J—and the fact that
I was an African American who had grown up in the hood. Phil
knew this would give me a kind of street cred that the players on
the team would respect.

Phil called me and told me in very general terms what he was
looking for, and I was hired on as a consultant to work with the
team in training camp, which started in October. Although the
Bulls consultancy was glamorous, it was only part-time. I still
needed to keep working at the Medical Center.

Phil and I knew that the team needed help, but we had to
figure out our approach on the fly. Wanting to help the players
help themselves, we simply made it up as we went along. That
openness, spontaneity, and playing by feel helped us get in touch
with what was real and true, helped us unlock the greatness inside

us and the players we were trying to help. We wanted to bring out the best in them, and when push came to shove, they knew that.

That isn't to say that it was easy; there were challenges. The NBA is a pressure cooker. Even though it's a sport, it's run as a business. The players are commodities and their value shifts, sometimes from game to game. Compared to most other jobs, many of the players are paid a fortune. But there are also many who are not. Some, like Bulls superstar and number-two option after Jordan, Scottie Pippen, were paid nowhere near what they were worth. Pippen was stuck in a bad contract even though he was a top-five player in the league at the time. Bulls management didn't want to pay him his market value until they absolutely had to. Needless to say, this created all kinds of turmoil and resentment. Dealing with and ameliorating those tensions was part of my job, and it was one wild ride.

PHIL HAD FREELY ADMITTED TO ME THAT THE TEAM WAS IN rough shape. We had a full-blown identity crisis on our hands, but I was determined. I knew that this was a made-in-heaven opportunity to fuse my two passions.

That's the way it is when we follow our heart, when we embrace what we feel most deeply and passionately about and let it guide us and shape our lives, no matter how improbable our path seems. Doors open where there were no doors. The universe colludes. My aunt Julia, who is very smart, an imam, said to me at the time: "You're doing what you were put here to do. You have answered your calling."

I flew to Chicago and went out to the team's new training facility in Deerfield, Illinois, a wealthy suburb about twenty-five miles north of the city. I soon learned that the distance between the training facility and the arena where the team played in Chicago was quite long, and the commute was a bear. The players lived near where they trained and had to get into the city for games, which was often a time-consuming challenge.

I had never even been to Chicago, let alone Deerfield, and it had been a while since I'd been around the game that I had devoted myself to as a kid and a young man. Here I was coming full circle, back to my first love, my initial passion—not as a player, but as something else that was hard to define. It made a kind of wonderful sense, and I knew that; yet, at the same time, I didn't know what to expect or how things would play out. Still, I was cautiously excited.

That is often the case with our biggest challenges and opportunities. If something doesn't make us feel that way, we're probably not in a situation that will foster optimal growth, one offering the fullest chance of unlocking and discovering the greatness within. Still, any new challenge can be harrowing. If we find ourselves in a harrowing situation, it's helpful to return to our original innocence, our basic kindness when we were children, when we were open and receptive and not full of ourselves, not trying to impose ourselves. Despite my cautious excitement, that is what I tried to do.

I reminded myself that I was there for a reason, and that reason was to help people help themselves; my task was to alleviate suffering and to share my experience, strength, and hope. What a great opportunity it was to get back in the game and to give back to the game that I loved! When we love something or someone, we help it grow, we nurture and take care of it, respecting it even as it is not as we might want it to be. We love what we labor for and we labor for what we love. The heart knows and love grows.

I knew that whatever was happening in the Bulls' training camp, it was not about me. I trusted that whatever I needed to say to the team would be useful and that whatever I needed to say would be given to me.

Phil just wanted me to work with them, to teach them how to deal with stress and give them a vision of possibility. He wanted them flow-ready, and he wanted me to do whatever it took to help get them there. We've all had flow experiences—experiences where we're optimally performing, totally immersed in the moment, doing and not thinking, and acting in alignment with some larger movement of life, whether it's the way a ten-foot wave is breaking as we surf down its steep face or putting together a complex business deal that seems to almost miraculously come together of its own accord.

My work with the Bulls didn't happen in a gym. We met in the media room of the training facility, which was like a small theater. This was the place where the team did their scouting reports and watched film. I was on stage for our sessions, and you can imagine how initially uncomfortable and self-conscious I felt. But I knew that Phil was behind me 100 percent. I strongly felt his support and friendship and belief.

"You've all had flow experiences," I told them after Phil introduced me. "I want to help you have more of those. Mindfulness gets you flow-ready. If you *try* to get into flow, it won't happen. But if you just attend to the moment—and if your challenges are high, and your skills, knowledge, and experience are all also high—you'll get there. It's a matter of continuing to push through and to challenge yourself."

I introduced them to the concept of being a spiritual warrior, explaining how that involved the conquest of the ego, the small self. You compete against your previous best self; the opponent is secondary. And I stressed the necessity of struggle and needing to get comfortable being uncomfortable. One side of the coin is freedom and potential; the other is uncertainty and anxiety. The Danish existential philosopher Søren Kierkegaard called it "the alarming possibility of being able." Anxiety must be accepted and fully experienced. As former poet laureate Robert Frost said, "The best way out is always through." As spiritual warriors, we have to train ourselves to overcome the internal obstacles and difficulties that stand in the way of allowing our latent abilities to express themselves. That is what unlocking is all about.

Now I see myself as incredibly naive. I make it sound as though I had very clear and well-developed ideas in mind that I brought to the Bulls players; I actually had absolutely no idea what I was doing. I was in the spirit. You have to understand—I used to be a very shy dude. It really helped that I was Black and had grown up in the hood. The players knew I was there to help them. And they knew Phil had a similar approach to helping

people. They could feel my authenticity and my willingness.
I created the opportunity for them to suspend disbelief and
see for themselves if what I was teaching was useful. This is a
very Buddhist concept. When people came to the Buddha and
challenged his teachings or asked why they should follow them
rather than all the other spiritual paths that were out there, he
encouraged them to try everything, to "see for yourself."

I was not allowed to take any photos or record any of the talks
I gave with any of the teams with whom I've worked. Privacy,
being in the moment, being able to be yourself—that was what
was crucial. Recording these sessions would have changed that.
I was working with a kind of alchemy. I had to have a pure
relationship with the players and with the work itself, where
I wasn't trying to use them and what went on between us to
promote myself. They needed to know that I was there to serve
them, and they needed to have absolute trust in that, in order
for them to open up and learn. In addition, I made sure that they
knew we were also there to have fun.

Initially I was on-site working with the team during training
camp, including their preseason games. I was then hired to
continue on into the regular season. I was in Illinois once a
month, five to ten days at a time, depending on their schedule.
During the playoffs, I was there more often.

Phil and I hit it off right away, and our relationship has only
grown tighter over the years. He took me to the LA Lakers with
him, and when he went to the New York Knicks, he took me

there as well. We remain good friends to this day. Not only did
I work with the players individually and collectively, I worked
with the coaches as well. That included Phil.

As I worked with the team, they got stronger. And not only
physically. They developed mental toughness, the ability
and willingness to push themselves and be comfortable with
discomfort. The meditation and stress reduction exercises we
worked through together helped them manage their emotions,
remain cool in the face of adversity, and keep a positive attitude.

We explored the two meanings of crisis: danger and opportunity.
"This is an opportunity for you to step up," I told them. This wasn't
anything they didn't know; they knew they would have to up their
game. They had been a supporting cast to Michael, appendages to
"His Airness," as he was often called in the press. This was a chance
for them to show what they could do on their own. Phil and I
didn't want to hear any excuses. If I had known my Vin Diesel in
those days, I would have said, "Step up or step aside."

And they responded. Even without Michael, the Bulls team of
1993–94, led by Scottie Pippen, won fifty-five games, swept the
Cleveland Cavaliers in the first round of the playoffs, and then
were defeated in the semifinals in a heartbreaker by the New
York Knicks in seven games. Those cats had everything to prove,
and they succeeded.

SIMILAR TO THE SHATTERING OF MY ANKLE IN COLLEGE AND MY
entry into detox, the period with the Bulls marked a turning point

in my life. I don't think it's a coincidence that I found my life partner during this period. I met Edye, who was in graduate school working toward her doctorate in psychology, just before I went to work with the Bulls in 1993, and I've been with her ever since.

Looking backward most of us can see a coherent shape to our lives. At the time, as we're living it, our day-to-day reality can feel as though it's one big scramble. We piece it together, reacting and responding as things come up. Trying to make sense.

People who say everything happens for a reason can be insufferable. But in a way it's true. There are periods in all our lives when things seem to come together in a way that defies explanation. There's a beautiful unfolding. And there are other periods when our lives fall apart. This is just the way it is— that law of averages again. It helps if we keep a Babe Ruth–like attitude. We may strike out this time up at the plate, and yet next time we go to bat there's a chance we'll crush it. In either case, we can strive to keep our mojo working and not be buffeted by circumstances or what people around us are saying. We can keep generating faith and hope.

Additionally, we can cultivate a conscious connection with a higher power, as we discussed earlier. If we do so, we will likely find ourselves aligning with what feels like "rightness" inside us. Prior to that point, we may feel that our lives lack direction and that the powers that be are in opposition to us—or, even worse, we may feel a kind of indifference, as though nothing and no one cared. When we cultivate conscious connection, doors will open where before there were no doors. It behooves us to accept this grace with humility. It has been said that the thing we fear most is our own power. That power is greater than we can comprehend. It is the movement and development of life itself. The way we can connect to it is by getting in touch with the love that is inside all of us, ready to be unlocked and flow.

Whatever we call it, and however we think about it and feel into it, we all want to be connected with something larger than ourselves. This is the path of unlocking, of coming into relationship with the greater movement of life, of being caught up in a power that is guiding and sustaining and illuminating and gives us a sense of our own strength and inimitable individuality. It is imperative to our happiness that we recognize and embrace our strengths and let go of the self-doubts we harbor, the fear that we are somehow unqualified or not enough.

Our feelings of insufficiency—which are counterfeit, given the love and power each of us contains—can be looked at in another way. From a Zen perspective, the divine essence within us could be thought of as nothing extra, as that which is perfectly ordinary, as nothing special. It is innately ours, existing always in us. We can never lose it. It is always available to us, right here, right now. Our task is to *recognize* it. The disciple asks the Zen master to teach her, to help her attain full realization, to finally know who and what she is, why she was born, and why she will die. "Have you had your lunch?" the Zen master asks. And with that, she is enlightened.

This is the path all of us are on, whether consciously or obliviously. We are all on the hero's journey, navigating our doubts and fears, slaying our dragons. We are all wondering about our meaning and purpose and trying, sometimes desperately, to find where we are strong, where we are most fully our best selves. We all are searching for ways to enter into flow, to swoop down the face of the wave, to feel in sync with the people around us, to lose ourselves in the joy and sublime challenge of being, and to feel connected with what is real and true.

PURE PERFORMANCE

The real risk is not changing. . . . It's the striving man, it's that I want.

—John Coltrane

I am often asked why I talk about "pure" performance rather than "peak" performance. After all, everyone wants to perform at their peak, to know what it is to finally achieve the summit and utilize latent capacities to their full potential. This is an understandable goal, but I think it's important for our well-being and growth that we modify it. Which is why I'm focused on "pure" rather than "peak."

What is the difference between peak performance and pure performance; and why should we concentrate, in whatever field we're in, on the latter? While peak performance is what people tend to strive for, one of its qualities is that it's inherently unsustainable. It doesn't promote growth, and it slides into an inevitable letdown eventually. In contrast, pure performance is about the quest for authenticity, which leads to purity of expression. There is no peak in pure performance, because there's no limit to the possibilities that exist. Peak performance is stationary—a mountain summit. Pure performance is flow, carrying us along ceaselessly and constantly revealing new heights, new possibilities, and new potential. Once we experience pure performance, we feel more fully ourselves and we want more.

This was one of Michael Jordan's secrets, perhaps the most important part of what made him so great, and it's a crucial part of what I taught him and also what he taught me. You can really explore the frontiers of talent and drive and the nature of competition with a guy like that. You can see what's possible in terms of our ability to keep growing and to sustain an unprecedented level of excellence.

People look at MJ's career, and they tend to point to fifty-point games and clutch shots and amazing defensive sequences and the airborne, otherworldly plays that he made, as though those were the pinnacles of his accomplishment. Fellow basketball legend Larry Bird famously said something like: That's not Michael Jordan—that's God disguised as Michael Jordan. And it's true—those games and plays and sequences *were* pinnacles, moments when we saw someone miraculously surpassing what we thought was possible. Those moments represented peak performance, to be sure. But MJ's virtuosity was also reflected in his consistently stellar level of performance over multiple seasons, and the complete aspect of his game: his ability to pass, rebound, and play defense as well as score. (The one aspect of his game that might be seen as less than elite was his three-point shooting, which was not as important when he played in the NBA as it is today.) That sustained excellence—that consistency, that breadth—is what distinguishes pure performance from peak performance. So how do we attain that? The question is similar to the question we explored in the previous chapter: How do we keep in constant contact with the greatness within and connect to whatever it is we might think of as a higher power?

MJ would come out of basketball retirement in March 1995 after a stint playing on the White Sox minor league baseball team. In explaining his shift to baseball, he said his father had always wanted him to be a professional baseball player, and he was dedicating himself to fulfilling his father's dream and honoring him. But then came the baseball lockout of 1995. MJ was afraid he might be named as a White Sox replacement player, and he didn't want to cross the picket line or go against the major league players' union. To our surprise and delight, he started showing up at the Bulls' training facility and participating in practices. Phil knew something was up, but we didn't dare hope. And then the second coming did, indeed, occur. "I'm back," MJ famously said in a press conference, adding that he had returned for "the love of the game."

President Bill Clinton joked that MJ's return to basketball would help the nation's employment figures. BJ Armstrong, who had played with the Bulls in their first three-peat before being traded to the Golden State Warriors and had stayed close to Jordan during his retirement from basketball, said he had seen the love for the game die in Jordan after his father's death. As MJ was coming back, he saw that love rekindled. Armstrong was quoted in the press as saying that he saw in Jordan, when he returned, an innocence and humility and a renewed sense of energy from missing being on the court.

We knew MJ's return was going to be a big deal, but that didn't prepare us for the eruption that happened. The media went wild, and the eyes of the world were suddenly focused on our team. The Bulls were nearing the end of a mediocre season at that point. We were thirty-one–thirty-one. It was unthinkable for MJ that the team might miss the playoffs. And indeed, even though he was rusty, without his basketball legs under him (baseball is a very different kind of sport), the Bulls won thirteen and lost only four games for the remainder of the season. We did make the playoffs, only to be dispatched in the first round, much to Michael's chagrin, by the Orlando Magic, who were led by a young Shaquille O'Neal.

I have no doubt MJ would have eventually succeeded in baseball. He was clearly getting better when he quit; he was beginning to play at a big-league level. Would he have been as good a baseball player as he was a basketball player? It's easy to scoff and say, *No way!* It would be wise, however, not to underestimate MJ. He had no ceiling. He was capable of doing things that hadn't been done before. He was like Roger Bannister, the runner who first broke the four-minute-mile barrier. People had said it couldn't be done. And then Bannister did it. The extreme sports people today— those snowboarders and skiers and big-wave surfers and free climbers and others who do seemingly impossible feats—show us that we are all capable of much more than we realize. Their example inspires us to push the envelope. They are about pure performance even though when they're engaged in what look like superhuman feats it seems as though they're peaking. It's actually part of a continuum to surpass and keep surpassing what they have previously achieved.

This was what MJ was all about. He was on a quest to keep improving. There was a famous "love of the game" clause in his contract with the Bulls that allowed him to play basketball at any time in any place with anyone. Usually when a player joins an NBA team, he is restricted from outside play, in large part due to the potential for injury. But one of MJ's stipulations was that he would not be constrained in that way. The love of the game defined him—the ability to play where he wanted, whenever he wanted.

MJ, like the athletes in extreme sports, was able to change what was possible. This is the essence of pure performance, and it exists inside each one of us. In pure performance, we transcend our limits again and again. Pure performance is not about specific moments of transcendence—the peaks, if you will—but about the process of becoming, of self-discovery, of finding out what we're made of and who we really are.

JUST DO

It was the second game after MJ came back to the team—we were in Boston to play the Celtics—that he first appeared at one of my pregame prep sessions. These were an essential part of my work with the Bulls. The team was staying at the Four Seasons. The hotel had supplied us with a small conference room where the team watched film with the coaches. When they were done, the coaches left. It was up to me to get the guys game-ready.

My pregame routine took about thirty minutes. First, I gave a little talk—one that varied each time depending on the mood of the room and what was needed in order to inspire them and center them and focus them on what was important. I'd read the "scout," which is what they called the game plan, but now wasn't the time to talk strategy; that wasn't my role. I talked instead about being alert, being relaxed. Being focused on the moment and making the next play. Not worrying about the longer term, the bigger picture. Just taking it one play at a time.

When I spoke to the team, I set an intention for the game and typically talked about embracing their own authentic way that they played the game, which needed not only mindfulness—being in the moment and focusing on the now—but *insight*.

"What is insight?" I might have said. "It's information, it's your discerning intellect working in accord with your intuition and your direct experience in the moment. Insight needs to be balanced with trust. Trust in yourself. Trust in the team. Trust in the game plan. Trust leads to faith, and faith is what you need in order to make right effort, which will lead to a good result. Your effort has to be based on insight and mindfulness of the moment, of what needs to be done *now*.

"What makes effort right? That it's coming from that place of stillness and emptiness that we touch when we meditate.

It comes out of the eye of the hurricane. That's where your authentic self is found and begins to express itself. Right effort needs to be balanced by concentration and poise. We need to be focused on the present moment, on what's happening in that present moment. This process gives us the opportunity to follow the game plan, see in real time how we're doing in relation to the game plan, and adjust what we're doing to achieve our goals."

Then—as was typical in my work with teams—we did a little chi kung, Chinese exercises that move energy through the body and focus the mind. This movement work was usually followed by breathing exercises. I had the players close their eyes and bring their awareness to the breath, breathing in and out into every part of their bodies from their heads to their toes. It's amazing how this helps to clear and focus the mind. And I wanted their minds clear, wanted them to have the experience of emptiness and be able to access the still point in the midst of the tremendous, swirling pace of the game. I wanted them to have the experience of the eye of the hurricane.

The repetition of the experience of accessing the still point—the eye of the hurricane—that comes through meditation makes it easier to access that place even when we're not meditating: when we're walking on a busy city street, preparing to walk on stage to deliver a presentation, being creative in whatever sphere we're in. Experienced meditators are able to slip into the eye of the hurricane no matter what's going on around them. The ability to do this helps athletes make plays and compete, remaining calm and focused and making decisions moment by moment from an unpressured and unperturbed place rather than being a bundle of nerves, reacting to what's being thrown at them at the breakneck pace of an NBA game (or whatever level they're playing).

In that first session with MJ, I joked that in these breathing exercises we were *conspiring*, from the Latin verb *spirare*, or "breath," and *con*, "with." *Conspire*, as we rendered it, was a word aligned with spirit and life itself. *One breath, one mind.*

I was very aware of MJ's presence that day. The aura around him was extremely strong. I've never felt anything like it. It was like coming into the gravitational field of a very large planet—Jupiter, for example. Matter bent toward him and around him. He created his own atmosphere. This was added to, of course, by his celebrity. He had an entourage of security whom he traveled with. They wore matching windbreakers. Whenever he was in public, he was recognized and approached. People wanted autographs and photos and just to be near him. He had tremendous patience with all this attention. He took the time necessary to interact with his fans, often staying for lengthy periods after games, signing autographs and appearing in photos. He had the patience of Job—it was one of his many remarkable qualities.

When he first came back to the team, I knew that MJ already knew who I was and why I'd been brought to the team. He knew my background in meditation and its application for dealing with stress, and he also knew about my relationship to Dr. J, who (it would be fair to say) was Michael Jordan before Michael Jordan. They had the same breathtaking razzle-dazzle in their games, and a similar type of celebrity, although Dr. J never approached MJ's status as the best-known person in the world. Nor did Dr. J have the opportunity to sign tremendously lucrative endorsement deals or to star in feature films (although he does appear on film, most recently in *Hustle*, starring Adam Sandler). The game had changed as MJ ascended to stardom, and MJ helped make the NBA a worldwide brand. It's hard to say how much of this would have happened without him. He was the face of the league. His superhuman abilities dazzled people from Topeka to Timbuktu.

I wasn't apprehensive, exactly, about how MJ would respond to what I was offering; at the same time, I was aware that he was coming in cold to something that the rest of the team had been practicing all season, and some of them for nearly two seasons now.

During the first part of the session, he was looking around to see how everyone else was conducting themselves. Then, when I asked the players to close their eyes and begin the awareness-of-breath exercises, something extraordinary happened. I could see that he just dropped right in. When you're experienced in teaching meditation, you can feel people's internal state as they meditate. You can see it in their posture and read it in the tension (or lack thereof) in their face muscles. You can hear it, like a score of music, in the quality of their breath. Both Michael and Kobe, the two greatest basketball players I ever worked with, were without question my best meditation students (along with those double lifers in the prisons). But this holds true as a general rule—the best athletes are also my best meditation students.

MJ just understood—immediately and intuitively—what meditation was all about, and the potential upside of making it part of the team's routine. He had already been introduced by Phil to some aspects of meditation, and now he was able to go deeper—to really make it a part of how he practiced and played and thought about the game.

I've often wondered with Michael and Kobe whether part of their genius was that they were so teachable. So *coachable*. They seemed to immediately see what you (as teacher or coach) saw, to understand the rationale for what you were trying to do. It went the other way as well. When you have receptive students, you become a better teacher. As a teacher, your most important attribute is to be able to see the potential in your students. To help them nurture their special gifts. To both encourage and challenge. When your students are open, you can more fully understand their special gifts. They are really the ones who make you see what is possible. And then you are able, in turn, to help *them* see it.

Teaching MJ and Kobe was exactly like that. They each had a very special kind of flexibility and open-mindedness. It might sound strange that when we're most in touch with who we really are, we're also at our most open. Our true, authentic self is not a fixed, unchanging thing. People who insist on defining themselves in that way tend to be rigid and self-defeating. We are fluid. In one sense, we are like chameleons. We do best when we allow the spontaneous expression of all the different selves that arise from the true self, that which makes us who we are and cannot be replicated, and which gives us an almost limitless ability to learn and grow.

Were MJ and Kobe great because they were so coachable or coachable because they were great? I've often thought about this and wondered. The lesson we can all take from them is to remain as open and flexible as possible. When we, the coaching staff, suggested that they do things differently, that they try a new approach that might up their game, they didn't get defensive. They really had what in Zen is called "beginner's mind."

Here's a brief version of a classic teaching story about that:

One day a Zen master was approached by someone who wanted to be his disciple. The would-be student impressed upon the master the great quality of his learning, the renowned teachers he had already studied with, and his knowledge of the sutras and other ancient texts.

"Would you like a cup of tea?" the master asked.

"Thank you," said the student.

The master poured the tea into a cup, and when it was full he kept pouring so that the tea spilled all over the table. How could the student learn if he was already so full of himself?

As Zen master Shunryu Suzuki said in *Zen Mind, Beginner's Mind*: "If your mind is empty, it is always ready for anything; it is open to everything. In the beginner's mind there are many possibilities; in the expert's mind there are few."

For all their dazzling accomplishments, MJ and Kobe had beginner's mind. They took what we offered and tried it out. If it worked, it worked; if not, they would try something else. They were always looking to grow and improve. That is the secret of pure performance.

When I watched Michael play, I noticed that one of his uncanny abilities was to become calmer as the game got more intense. It was almost as if the pressure comforted him. Perhaps the pressure created a kind of swaddling. His concentration and focus increased. He entered the eye of the hurricane. While the storm raged around him, he was in a place of placid stillness.

KOBE WAS A BLACK MAMBA, BUT MICHAEL WAS CATLIKE. HE moved with deadly feline grace. In today's aerial game, people are always crashing to the floor and being helped up by their teammates. Not MJ. He rarely fell, although he was always leaping. He landed on his feet, just like a cat.

MJ never took a day off. Not one. He was always connected to spirit, though he didn't need to go to church to accomplish that. Spirit was already inside him. He had an attitude and philosophy about life that saw him as *earning* everything. He wasn't asking anybody to *give* him anything. He practiced with exactly the same level of intensity and competitive fire with which he played. He was the best player in the league, maybe the greatest of all time. But he was *always* working. We can all learn from that kind of relentless drive and consistency of effort about the nature of pure performance: it comes with total commitment and grueling work. Even at MJ's level: no struggle, no swag.

MJ practiced the way he played because it all mattered equally to him. When he took the court, opponents knew they were in trouble. He was going to be a problem. It didn't matter who he was up against. There was nothing casual about him. That's just the way it was.

Phil was always looking to help the team get to higher and higher levels of *wellness*. That was the ultimate goal—winning was a by-product. The way we measure pure performance is against our personal best. Phil wanted that for the team. Phil didn't stress winning so much as wanting his players to be the best possible versions of themselves—to *find themselves* in the game. He stressed that the way to do this was by working together, by dropping the "me" in favor of the "we." One could think of the analogy of five fingers of one's hand, all working together. The fingers are moving but they are connected, directed by something larger than each finger individually.

Phil and I worked with the dynamic tension between the me and the we. It's a delicate balance that all of us—in one way or another in whatever sphere of life we're in—are always managing. One of the great things about working with Phil was that he also held the attitude of beginner's mind. We were both always evolving in our own thinking, continuing to read, learn, and explore. We frequently gave the players new ideas, new perspectives, books to read, and ideas to consider. As noted, Phil believed that it was crucial to develop the "whole person," not just the athlete.

The proof was in the pudding during the 1995–96 season. MJ came to training camp in the fall of 1995 in incredible shape; having worked hard since his return the previous March, he again had his basketball legs fully under him. We won seventy-two games with only ten losses, which at that time was an NBA record for most wins in a season. That record has since been broken by the Golden State Warriors, with seventy-three wins. (The Warriors, not coincidentally, are coached by Steve Kerr, one of the players on the Bulls team of that year, who has gone on to be a tremendously successful coach.)

We worked our asses off that season, but it was a hell of a lot of fun. Everybody was pulling for the same thing, and the team did run like a well-oiled machine. Phil wrote about that season in his book *Sacred Hoops*: "The Bulls found a rhythm with which to play and win convincingly during the 1995–6 season. I tried very hard to keep the focus of the season on just winning games and not getting caught up in numbers. I stressed: come to work each day because it is important to do it right; do each action with conscious effort. That is what we do: chop wood, carry water. We tried to play each play in every game and not let the games play us."

Doing each action with conscious effort is part of pure performance. When people talk to me about wanting to function at a high level in whatever they're doing, and they ask me to guide them there, I tell them that there is no peak—don't be aiming for a peak. When we're performing at our highest level, we're doing what we're doing with conscious effort but for no particular reason. In other words, we're not focused on outcome or trying to prove people wrong or trying to convince people that we're good. Our performance is authentic and sincere. Bruce Lee said that the martial arts are about honestly expressing ourselves. When they're not about that, their spirit is false. They are no longer the martial *arts*, and we might even say that what they become is bereft of beauty and dignity. That is always the case when we're acting and creating as a means to an ego-driven end.

Honestly expressing ourselves is about being fully engaged. We express what's inside us for no particular reason other than the joy of the moment. We don't withhold. We just focus on doing the task at hand to the best of our ability. We do what we're doing. Make a pass, set a screen, negotiate a contract, sing a lullaby to our child before bed, write an email—it doesn't matter. Be in touch with your authentic self. That is what the Zen saying that Phil quotes—*chop wood, carry water*—conveys. Just do. Don't second-guess yourself. It's not that our wants and needs aren't real. But there is also a deeper reality at work, and we need to come into tune with that as well as taking care of ourselves. And as we experience that deeper reality and our authentic self, as we come into accord with them, we find that our needs get taken care of in a way that is often new and wonderful.

PURE PERFORMANCE AND THE AUTOTELIC PERSONALITY

Another way to think about pure performance is that it's the result of what's called an "autotelic personality," a term that comes out of the psychology of flow. Someone with an autotelic personality undertakes an activity for its own sake, not for other means. "Autotelic" also applies to an activity or endeavor done for the sake of the experience and not some other goal. Whether we apply "autotelic" to a person or an activity, we mean the same thing: the doing is its own reward. It is not a means to an end. The goal of the activity has nothing to do with anything outside oneself. To play or work or live in an autotelic way means that the joy of accomplishment, or end result, and the joy in doing whatever it is we're doing in the moment are indistinguishable. Chop wood, carry water. Very simple. But often not easy.

That does not mean we stomp out any vestige of intention. On the contrary. We set our intention for what we want. But then we execute the intention in a way that we're going to feel good about from start to finish. Autotelism is a clean-burning fuel. There is no detritus, no residue. No smudge of ego. We could be performing and still lose, which is what basketball great Bill Russell noted in the passage from his book that I quoted earlier. It's important to set goals, and it's equally important to be able to let them go and just manage the moment. It's the same way of being that we discussed above—to just *do*. When we're in flow, in the zone, our sense of self-consciousness evaporates, and something larger than ourselves begins to reveal itself through us.

Michael would say that during a game he was "just playing," which was his way of saying he was chopping wood and carrying water. He was getting out of his own way, which allowed extraordinary things to happen. I saw Dr. J go through something similar. When he played his first semipro game, I was there. And he was suddenly making moves that he'd never made before. Which I recognized because I knew his game inside out: I had often shared the court with him and also frequently watched him play. He was breaking ground, discovering himself, cutting loose from where he had been before.

Is there anything more exciting in life than to have that kind of experience? We're suddenly in unexplored terrain, a whole new country opening up. What allows that to happen? Luck? I don't think so. The possibilities for newness come when we are able to let go of or transcend our conditioning, the subtle and not so subtle messages that have lodged inside us regarding what we're capable of. The constant evaluative measures that have been foisted on us, and which we have foisted on others. Or, perhaps most injurious, that we have foisted on ourselves. Is there anything more pernicious? More deadening of spirit and spontaneous joy? Do we think, Oh well, that's just the way things are? Is it? Really?

The spiritual teacher Adyashanti writes in *The End of Your World*: "This isn't a journey about becoming something. This is about *unbecoming who we are not*, about undeceiving ourselves. In the end, it's ironic. We don't end up anywhere other than where we have always been, except that we perceive where we have always been completely differently. We realize that the heaven everyone is seeking is where we have always been."

The heaven Adya is talking about is not a static thing. It does not emerge and become present just during meditation or other so-called spiritual pursuits or activities. It is active. It is about doing. The full expression of our authentic self, of who we really are, is paradoxical. It is autotelic, and yet we are playing our part in the unfolding of life, in being and becoming. There is a feeling of oneness, of divine union, and yet we also feel most fully ourselves. It is an experience of intimacy, of entering the flow of life so that there is not separation between you and the ten thousand things.

That is what MJ embodied when he played. It was his gift to the world, and the world and the accolades and the wealth the world gave back were really just a way of saying thank you.

OUR GREAT TALENTS ARE ALWAYS AUTOTELIC. MJ'S "LOVE OF THE game" clause in his contract came from that place. Once we've unlocked and touched the greatness within, we see that there's nothing more important. It is *everything*.

Life is never really about winning or losing: it's about playing the right way. The love of the game was what was most important to MJ, even though he wanted to win at everything all the time, perhaps more than anyone else I've ever met. His competitive fire was at the core of who he was. His drive to win was relentless.

There's a great scene in *The Last Dance*, the Netflix ten-episode documentary about Michael Jordan and the story of the Chicago Bulls' six NBA championship titles (which was brilliantly spoofed by Keegan-Michael Key in a *Saturday Night Live* skit), where MJ is pitching quarters with one of his security guards, John Michael Wozniak. The person who can get the quarter closest to the wall wins twenty dollars. Jordan loses to Wozniak, and you can see how pissed MJ is—the loss obviously irks. Wozniak, on the other hand, looks like the cat that ate the canary. Taking twenty bucks off Michael Jordan—the GOAT and your boss to boot. Could anything be sweeter? The point of the scene is not only how hard Jordan took the loss, but that he would compete anywhere at any time with anyone. The will to win was always active in him and ready to assert itself. When people accused Jordan of having a gambling problem, his reply was that he didn't have a gambling problem—he had a *competition* problem.

There are many stories that illustrate MJ's competitive fervor. To offer only one more example: MJ got his ass whupped at Ping-Pong by Christian Laettner, according to a story on sportscasting.com. Jordan reacted by throwing down his paddle. He then refused to talk to anyone for two days. Over losing a game of Ping-Pong! He didn't take the loss sitting down, however. He had a Ping-Pong table delivered to his hotel room and worked on his game for two days straight, emerging for a rematch where he held his own.

MJ, Kobe—they both had a killer instinct. The will to win. Most elite performers and their coaches credit success to the desire to succeed. MJ and Kobe had that desire more than most. It was reflected in their willingness to work hard and use obstacles and difficulties as stepping-stones. Where most people would walk away or say it didn't matter, these cats saw opportunity and an invigorating challenge.

When we talk about pure performance in conjunction with MJ, with the letting go of ego and being in the moment and the flow of the game, it's important to remember that MJ's intention was always set, and that intention was to *win*.

It is a fine line between balancing the me and the we, which we have already discussed. How should we approach the balance that exists in pure performance between the killer instinct—that competitive edge we need to play or work at our highest level—and autotelism, the entry into flow to which we all aspire? I don't think it has to be one or the other. Both these parts of us can exist simultaneously. It is the tension between them that propels performers like MJ and Kobe. We need both seemingly opposing principles. They are reconciled when we direct our activities toward service, toward giving back, realizing that what we manage to accomplish is not about gratifying our ego and pumping ourselves up. It is our connection with the greatness within that unlocks pure performance and gives life its richness and meaning.

PEAK EXPERIENCES AND PURE PERFORMANCE

The "peak performance" label was co-opted from the work of positive psychologist Abraham Maslow, who talked about "peak experiences." Those terms are not interchangeable, however. In fact, Maslow's "peak experiences" are closer to what we mean when we talk about "*pure* performance."

The experience of being in the zone or flow is a peak experience, and it is also an expression of pure performance. In a flow state, we have the ability to intend some action and allow it to unfold of its own accord. There is no self-consciousness; no fear, no desire. Despite being in the eye of the hurricane, we can observe the action calmly and be like water, flowing with the current in a way that seems effortless; yet we also experience a knowing that comes out of the eye of the hurricane, out of the silence, that's spot on: on time and on point.

Pure performance and flow are about allowing what wants to happen to happen, and so are what Maslow described as peak experiences. In peak experiences—sometimes also called "peak states of consciousness"—we feel taken over by something larger than ourselves; sometimes we feel that we've touched the ineffable, communed with the divine. Maslow defined peak experiences as "powerful, meaningful experiences in which individuals seem to transcend the self, be at one with the world, and feel completely self-fulfilled."

In his book *Toward a Psychology of Being*, Maslow identified sixteen aspects of peak experiences, many of which are more or less present in pure performance:

1. Sense of unity of the self

2. Oneness with the environment

3. Experience of peak power

4. Non-forcing, or unforced effort

5. Self-determination

6. Freedom from inhibition

7. Spontaneity

8. Purposeless creativity

9. Timelessness

10. Pinnacle of individuality

11. Merging of I and other

12. Non-need motivation

13. Artistic expression

14. Sense of completion

15. Playfulness

16. Surprise happenings

Many of these sixteen aspects of peak experience can be cultivated through daily rituals and mental training, which is what Phil and I were working toward with the Bulls in the late 1990s, during the years of their second three-peat.

The language that I use in discussing the idea of pure performance comes from the words of the Buddha, who spoke of his transmission of mindfulness as being for the "purification of all beings." What did he mean by that? Is it a religious concept, perhaps associated as it is in the West with abnegation and the ethereal, making it a kind of prissiness that doesn't want to get its hands dirty or muck around in the mud of quotidian reality and base human impulses? Is it purity as transcendence, a leaving of this imperfect world with all its struggle and strife and inevitable compromises and imperfections behind?

Although there may be undertones of that in the purification of which the Buddha speaks, what we're concentrating on here is a refinement of behavior so that it expresses our authenticity, is a spontaneous reflection of who we really are. There is nothing added, no overlay—thus it is pure. When we're most truly ourselves, we display effortless effort. The snow naturally slips from the bamboo leaf and the leaf springs back. The arrow finds its target in the dark. We score without trying to score. We feel most fully ourselves: not some washed out, scrubbed clean, disinfected, whitewashed angelic epitome of goodness and virtue. What we are is perfectly natural—nothing artificial or affected. We're not pushing an agenda or trying to make something happen. Life is happening in us and through us. We have the kind of childlike innocence that I mentioned earlier, which Maslow referred to as playfulness, spontaneity, and purposeless creativity. We become again like children, having the gift of being in the moment—without filters, with no other intention than to express ourselves. Pure performance is rare: there is no "I" present—at least, not in the way we usually think about the self. The child at play is in her own autotelic universe. There is trust, as though she were letting the current carry her. She is lost in a realm of pure imagination.

What does that look like in an adult? Well, it looks like MJ and his love of the game. Or an artist lost in her art. It can also exist irrespective of activity, simply as a way of life. Trudy Dixon, a student of Shunryu Suzuki, the author of *Zen Mind, Beginner's Mind* (referenced earlier), in the prefatory material to that book, describes what it was like to be around Suzuki:

> He [Suzuki] exists freely in the fullness of his whole being. The flow of his consciousness is not the fixed repetitive patterns of our usual self-centered consciousness, but rather arises spontaneously and naturally from the actual circumstances of the present. The results of this in terms of the quality of his life are extraordinary—buoyancy, vigor, straightforwardness, simplicity, humility, serenity, joyousness, uncanny perspicacity and unfathomable compassion. His whole being testifies to what it means to live in the reality of the present. . . . In his presence we see our own original face, and the extraordinariness we see is only our own true nature.

To live in the reality of the present. That is perhaps the closest rendition of the meaning of "purification" in the Buddha's words above. As Pema Chodron says: "Right down there in the thick of things, we discover the love that will not die."

In the passage about Suzuki quoted above, Dixon is drawing "see our own original face" from a well-known Zen koan that goes like this: *What is your original face before your parents were born?* Our original face is the authenticity of pure performance. It is the greatness within. Watching MJ play, that's what I felt; the authenticity and greatness were palpable. That's why the great basketball player Larry Bird said what he said about watching MJ play—that God was disguised as Michael Jordan.

And MJ brought the team along with him. Pure performance can be contagious. It generates a spell that others fall under. When we're under it, the spell can feel eternal and all-encompassing. But it is, by its nature, fragile. If we call attention to it or try to analyze it—poof, it's gone. Language can't really describe it. It must be experienced. We know it when it's happening, and it feels precious, like the awe-inspiring peak experiences that Maslow describes. We really do become again like little children in their innocence and purity. We play for the sake of playing, for the "love of the game." It feels like a homecoming, a return to a state with which we were familiar but somehow strayed from or lost. As the poet T. S. Eliot wrote in "The Four Quartets": "We shall not cease from exploration, and the end of all our exploring will be to arrive where we started and know the place for the first time."

MJ WAS THE POSTER CHILD FOR WHAT I'M TEACHING: unlocking and uncovering the greatness within. For me to be able to work with him—to teach him—I had to communicate that great as he was, there was another level to be attained. This didn't put him off. He had beginner's mind and was always up for improvement, for doing whatever it took to get better. What I was doing was not just about upping his game—it was about helping him better understand himself. That's one of the most important adventures we can have. Not simply to understand our quirks and personality or the nuances of our motivation. Those things are interesting and important, yes—but they're not the crucial task. What I mean is *knowing our essence*, and *that* is not subject to analysis. Our hearts speak to us in this language. But we need to listen.

It's hard to hear our hearts speaking if we screen everything through the shell of our conditioning. Yet letting go of conditioning—which encompasses the familiar and expected— often involves anxiety. The ground feels as though it's been pulled out from under us. In some ways, learning their essence, finding their inner greatness—achieving pure performance—is what MJ encouraged his teammates to do: he inspired them to work as hard as he did, to have the same fire and drive. That wasn't possible, of course, because he did vibrate on another level; he was utterly and unapologetically relentless.

It's not as though we can force someone to be that way. Parents who try to do that with their kids and coaches who try to do it with players are ultimately frustrated and disappointed. The will and drive have to come organically from within. MJ's attitude was that if his teammates didn't want to mirror his work ethic and level of intensity, they should go elsewhere. He wanted to bring people on board who were hungry. Players who were never satisfied and who wanted to keep winning by surpassing themselves. He wanted teammates who were interested not in peak performance but in pure performance.

The nature of healthy competition is that we bring out the best in each other. This is not a Darwinian model of dog-eat-dog survival of the fittest. It's true that MJ had the killer instinct, yet as much as he hated losing, he did not objectify his opponents. We need to avoid objectification too. Healthy competition does not make our opponent into a "thing."

There is no "enemy" out there, in the world of pure performance: we are competing with—not against—our previous best selves. The aim is to get better little by little, expanding our capacity, getting out of our comfort zone, getting comfortable being uncomfortable. That is the warrior spirit. The spiritual warrior sees the opponent as deeply respected, there to make us better, to help us along the way of self-knowledge and bring us closer to the truth and the greatness within. Life is seen as a series of challenges to be embraced. Challenges are necessary obstacles and difficulties. The spiritual warrior uses them as stepping-stones to move to ever greater levels of self-knowledge and awareness.

Productive competition involves always recognizing our opponent's humanity. What I mean by that is not just that we are all human, though we are. Beyond that—far beyond—each of us is endowed with divinity.

Each one of us is a child of God. We are all emanations of creation, and we are connected to each other in this way. Each one of us is essential and irreplaceable. When Bill Russell talks about the prescient nature of pure performance (knowing what everyone is going to do before they do it), this is what he is recognizing—our interconnection, and the causes and conditions and codependent arising of phenomena (to use Buddhist terms) that give rise to our reality moment to moment.

In pure performance, it's as though a veil had been removed. What had been opaque clarifies. The underlying mechanisms that govern reality become clear—how one moment leads to the next; how one action affects the whole, affects the underlying architecture of existence, if you will.

In *peak* performance, our intention may be to crush our opponent. The tapestry and its underlying structure of relationships don't matter to us in that moment. We just want to get to the top, to the peak. We want to prevail in our one little corner of what is. How small-minded and selfish! This is not the way of the spiritual warrior and pure performance. We relish the contest first and foremost for the ways in which it helps us enter into a larger appreciation of reality, to know ourselves more fully, to come into conscious connection with the greatness within.

Our world today is stingingly partisan and fraught. So much of everyday life is about winning at all costs by whatever means necessary. We demonize other people and ideas. The air is infused with an acrid nastiness. How can we mean what we say without being mean? How can we create a culture where we're willingly generous enough to do things that will advance the greater good? The first step is to go within and discover what's really inside us, who we really are—our essence. There's a whole universe inside each one of us, and more profound discoveries waiting to be made there than anywhere else.

In the eighteen months MJ was away from the team, they'd learned how to function with some degree of success without him. When he came back, it was a huge change: his teammates had to exercise parts of themselves that had been latent and unexpressed. They had to learn to stop watching him to see what he was going to do and then simply react. They had to work to be able to come into the moment and actually participate and play with him, which is no easy task when you have someone of MJ's caliber. They had to be the other fingers on the hand, moving with him as he moved in what was, during that remarkable 1995–96 season, a telepathic choreography that was—as is always the case in the highest level of sports or any other performative activity— unrelentingly improvisational and unexpected. Something new and fresh was always coming into being. Which is what made that record-breaking season so thrilling. It was not just MJ who dazzled and showed the world what pure performance was all about—it was the entire team. It was the *we*.

It's important that we remember that we set up the conditions for flow-readiness and pure performance through deliberate *practice*, whether that's repeating scales on the piano or practicing our crossover on the basketball court or undertaking a spiritual practice. Practice is always just that—the way to make deliberate and conscious connection with what is good and true inside us. Productive practice does not involve mindless repetition. That kind of repetition is the opposite of what it means to be mindful. To be deliberate means to do whatever it is that we're doing *with conscious intention*. We have to be able to sustain focus and concentration and not let whatever it is that we're practicing become rote. We want to stay present and focused.

Martial arts master Bruce Lee said: "I fear not the man who has practiced 10,000 kicks once, but I fear the man who has practiced one kick 10,000 times." It's by doing repetitions that we learn. It's a circular process. We repeat the same task again and again and again, picking up new information and intelligence each time, although this learning process can often be subtle, implicit, perhaps even unconscious.

World champion bodybuilder, movie star of *Terminator* fame, and former governor of California Arnold Schwarzenegger said that lifting one weight with total consciousness is equal to ten lifts with less than total consciousness. That's a very powerful statement. To be fully in the present moment, to have total consciousness, is what pure performance is all about, whether we are stretched beyond our limits of energy and endurance in the final quarter of a close game in the NBA finals, negotiating a raise at work, playing a complex and challenging passage of a piano concerto, or washing the dinner dishes with presence and deliberate attention. All things, experienced in this way, are equally valid and important. In pure performance it's not necessarily what we do; it's how we do it. All of life is about chopping wood and carrying water. Pure performance is very simple and very ordinary. It is the state we were all born into and to which we seek to return.

Chop wood, carry water. We want to get to the point where winning and losing, although they can be important, are ultimately not what matters most. What matters most is the doing of the thing. Or, as MJ said most eloquently, the love of the game.

ABIDING IN LOVE

Impossible is just a big word thrown around by small men who
find it easier to live in the world they've been given than to explore
the power they have to change it. Impossible is not a fact. It's an
opinion. Impossible is not a declaration. It's a dare. Impossible
is potential. Impossible is temporary. Impossible is nothing.

—Muhammad Ali

The magnificent 1995–96 season with the Bulls led to the first
of their second three-peat championships. Those three years
for me were truly amazing—it was like touring with the Rolling
Stones. Everywhere we went, hundreds of people swirled around
us in a giddy frenzy.

Phil and MJ left the Bulls after the 1997–98 season, and then
Phil was hired by the Los Angeles Lakers in 1999. He brought
me back into the game with him, and I found myself doing my
thing with Kobe and Shaq. LA, not surprisingly, was a different
vibe with new challenges. I don't want to compare the Lakers and
the Bulls, which feels like a parent comparing one of his kids to

another. Not a cool thing to do. And I can't say too much about the inside workings of either team. There's a code of decorum at work, which really exists in all professions but is particularly important in professional sports—especially in the intimate work I did with the players.

But the two environments—Chicago and LA—*were* different. What I will say is that working for the Bulls was like being strapped to a rocket ship, blasting into orbit. MJ was the most famous person in the world, and he and the Bulls had turned basketball into a worldwide phenomenon and the NBA upside down. That wasn't really the scene with the Lakers. You go into the Staples Center and what you feel is not only the glamour and star power of Hollywood, but a long tradition of polish, excellence, and winning. There is an excitement at Staples that has its own particular kind of effervescence and charisma, and it was different than the juggernaut that was Michael Jordan's Bulls.

THE INNER GAME OF LIFE

Phil would stay with the Lakers through 2011 (with a brief hiatus) and win five more NBA championships; I still worked with the team, but my life and work encompassed far more than that. I was committed to serving wherever I could, teaching mindfulness, stress reduction, team building, unlocking, and accessing the masterpiece within to a variety of clients.

At the University of Massachusetts Medical Center in Worcester, Massachusetts, I developed and implemented mindfulness-based stress reduction programs for an inner-city "satellite" clinic along with the prisons, and I also presented conferences, including "Alternative and Integrative Medicine for Pain Management," sponsored by the health system at the University of California, Davis; and "Leading from Within," sponsored by the University of Pennsylvania, Wharton School of Business. One of the most exciting invites was being asked to participate in the "Healing Through Great Difficulty" conference, which was described as "a meeting between His Holiness the Dalai Lama and former prisoners and meditation teachers." I also taught at spiritual centers, including the Cambridge Insight Meditation Center (CIMC), the Insight Meditation Society (IMS), Spirit Rock, the Omega Institute, and the Kripalu Center for Yoga and Health. In addition, I gave lectures, workshops, and seminars on team development for a variety of organizations.

Through all of these activities, I continued to refine what I wanted to convey. Fortunately, it was a good time to be doing what I was doing. The business world was beginning to take a keen interest in how the field of sports psychology could help organizations up the performance of both employees and management. And schools were interested in new ways not only to improve their sports programs but to help kids cope with stress and gain confidence.

Then, in 1997, Timothy Gallwey's book *The Inner Game of Tennis* was reissued and made waves. The book was about much more than tennis, just as *Zen in the Art of Archery* is about much more than hitting the bull's-eye. *The Inner Game* was essential reading if you were a serious tennis player. But the reason it drew a readership beyond tennis and spawned a whole new way of thinking of performance generally was because it showed that the quality of the outer game—serve, volley, ground stroke—was *always* a reflection of the inner game: in other words, our outer game is a reflection of what's going on in our heads.

Gallwey, who had been a nationally ranked player and had become a sought-after coach, wrote that the aspiring players he taught frequently engaged in self-sabotage by relying on thinking instead of just doing, by trying to control the learning process of hitting shots with their heads instead of with the far more effective intuitive intelligence that existed in their bodies. He taught a learning that happened unconsciously, that wasn't willed. In one sense, Gallwey was going over the same ground that Herrigel had covered; but instead of showing how these insights played out in a Zen setting in faraway Japan with people performing esoteric rituals while wearing elaborate, formal kimonos, Gallwey's book took place in town and country tennis clubs with people dressed in Ralph Lauren and Nikes. The book was a huge success when reissued, and suddenly everybody wanted coaching on the inner game, which is exactly what I was teaching.

GALLWEY WROTE THAT THE FIRST SKILL NEEDED TO DEVELOP THE inner game is the art of letting go of "the human inclination to judge ourselves and our performance as either good or bad. Letting go of the judging process is a basic key to the Inner Game. . . . When we *unlearn* how to be judgmental, it is possible to achieve spontaneous, focused play." This struck me as quite similar to the Buddhist teaching that I had learned and experienced in Vipassana meditation and which I now taught. I wanted to make explicit, in a way that hadn't been done in quite the way I wanted to do it, how the psychology of meditation and performance in sports and elsewhere are intimately linked.

The process of "unlearning judging" that Gallwey notes above is also similar to what I learned through experience. We followed the movement of the mind away from negatively perceived stimuli or objects (an unpleasantly blaring car horn, for example) toward something perceived as pleasant (the delicious dinner we're looking forward to), or toward something to which the mind is neither attracted nor averse. We're almost always unconsciously involved in this kind of evaluative process—one that judges things bad or good—with detrimental effects. That process keeps us from being fully in the moment. It is as though we were only half alive.

This is typically what's happening behind the scenes when things aren't flowing on the basketball court or in a company trying to market or sell a new product. We're somehow getting tripped up in our head. The energy is askew or dulled. In flow, the energy doesn't have to do with stressing and straining and reacting and panting and pushing and forcing. No! The snow slips from the leaf and the leaf springs back; the arrow shoots itself; we are carried by the current. The intelligence of the body takes over and the decisions we're making in our mind about what to do next bloom inside us naturally and spontaneously. And *inevitably*. "Oh yes," we think. "How could it be any other way? This is the way it's supposed to be." That's what it means to be unlocked.

INSTILLING STRESS HARDINESS AND CONFIDENCE IN KIDS

Through my own evolution and teaching, I fell on a metaphor that works beautifully as a way to understand the pace of our existence: life is like a marathon, and we have to train for it in the same way an athlete trains. We are all searching to find our rhythm in the same way that the long-distance runner seeks to establish a sustainable pace. Start off too fast and we'll be winded with miles to go; we'll collapse before we cross the finish line. Start off too slowly and we may eventually finish, but we'll be so far behind that we won't qualify.

Finding the right pace and a rhythm to our life is essential. Can we identify our own rhythm? Can we feel how we're at our best when we move through life at a certain pace? Can we gauge when we're giving an appropriate amount of energy to any given task, as well as when we're overextended? This kind of pace or rhythm exists at the micro level too, in the pacing of each breath. When we become aware of the breath, we are on our way to becoming aware of our internal rhythm, the pace at which our life wants to move. And when we become aware of our breath, through the breathing techniques we've already discussed, we can learn to regulate our rhythm and live in a way that helps us feel balanced and present in the moment while also helping us achieve our long-term goals.

In all our activities, how can we train deliberately, consciously, efficiently like an athlete? It's a truism in basketball that the way you practice is the way you play. That is one of the reasons that

MJ's savage, explosive practices were so amazing to watch. Not only was he leaving it all on the floor at each practice, but—as we saw earlier—he insisted that the whole team join him at his level of intensity. The practice wasn't about getting ready for the main event. Every time he took the court—any court, anywhere— *that* was the main event; it was of supreme importance and consequence. Every activity was the same activity. Chop wood, carry water. It was part of his commitment to an unbroken continuum that was about improving the full range of his elite skills, both as an individual player and as part of his team.

Along with developing an inner pace or rhythm, we also need to craft a strategy for overcoming adversity. I find this particularly important when I work with kids, who often struggle not to feel defeated by what they perceive as their failures. It is a chronic problem—and not *just* with kids.

Many of us feel that we're lurching from one mistake and one failed opportunity to the next. Indeed, during my alcoholic and drug-addled years, that was the way I felt: as though I were being propelled against my will into an abyss. That experience of being out of control turned out to be incredibly useful, however—it allowed me to surrender. Because I had been in the thrall of something more powerful than I was, that I was helpless against, I knew what it was to give myself over to a higher power. Addiction was the crude, destructive version of what became fundamental to my recovery. The higher power in recovery can be anything that connects us to the whole, to life, and to each other. We make that connection when we feel that we're part of something larger than ourselves. When the ego recedes and the *me* comes into balance with the *we*. When that happens, we breathe a sigh of relief and of profound recognition. It is a homecoming, a return to the koan's "original face." *Chop wood, carry water*. Very simple. But not easy. The mind is always tripping us up.

Sports psychologists study what's called "error attribution." It's an easy enough concept to grasp. When we make a mistake, what do we attribute our error to? The novice or amateur tends to attribute errors to some fault: I am not fast enough, strong enough, smart enough. The elite performer, however, tends instead to attribute errors to lack of *sustained effort*. Instead of withdrawing energy and getting defensive about mistakes, the elite performer brings more energy to bear, using all her resources to figure out how things work and aligning herself with that. In mindfulness training, we call this "right effort," a concept we touched on earlier.

Right effort is based on wisdom, on understanding. We realize— like the meditation-ready double lifers in the prisons where I taught—that *we* are responsible, no one else. We are responsible for how we react to screwing up and to whatever life throws at us, no matter how seemingly unfair. It always starts with us, with the individual self.

ADDRESSING ERROR ATTRIBUTION IN THE CONTEXT OF RIGHT effort, we develop what's called "stress hardiness." The stress that comes with challenges and hardship is crucial for growth. We just have to know how to use it positively.

This is a lesson best learned young, which is why I take every opportunity I can to work with kids, generally in schools or in sports programs. To illustrate stress hardiness with a group of younger kids, I often tell them the story of the caterpillar undergoing metamorphosis inside a chrysalis. It is quite a job for this plump little creature to turn itself into a butterfly, break through the chrysalis, and find its way into the world. It has to work hard.

One day, a little boy finds the chrysalis in the forest and takes it home. He is excited to help. Seeing the little caterpillar inside, he takes a scissors and cuts open the chrysalis so that the little bug can come out. But when the caterpillar emerges, it's ill-formed, too heavy for its body. The caterpillar falls to the ground and then dies.

"What do you think the story means?" I ask the kids. "What's the lesson here?"

"You've got to do it for yourself," I remember one young girl saying. "No one can make you into a butterfly."

"That's exactly right," I said, glad that the message had gotten through. "The lesson is that it is by struggling to get out of the chrysalis that you build the strength to fly. I'm sorry to say it's the same for all of us. You have to build yourselves up. You have to know adversity in order to become strong inside."

There is an important distinction between *stress* and its counterpart, *eustress*. Eustress is the positive aspect of moderate stress, which has a beneficial effect on health, motivation, performance, and emotional well-being. We need eustress—in the form of challenges—in order to grow. The struggle to break free of the chrysalis is what strengthens and forms us.

Stress hardiness comes from being able to separate stimulus from response. I explain to the kids: "You can watch your own behavior, your own reactions. Say someone does something mean to you. You can develop the ability to look at yourself from inside, to step back inside yourself and see how you're reacting to that meanness. You can observe yourself. You can feel curious about why you're reacting in a way that feels hurt, insulted, or vengeful. You can develop an inner witness to your actions that has the ability to say, 'Wait a minute, slow down, don't jump the gun. Chill!'"

This concept is particularly difficult for younger kids, who are naturally impulsive and uninhibited. "You are not your thoughts," I tell the kids. "Our thoughts are just a story we're telling ourselves. Our thoughts are based on all kinds of assumptions. We say 'I'm angry' or 'I'm sad.' But is this really who we are? Our feelings are like the weather. One day it's raining; the next, it's sunny. By witnessing our behavior from the inside, we can see that our thoughts and feelings are just information we can use to understand ourselves. When we learn to look at where those thoughts and feelings and the stories we tell ourselves are coming from, we see that they come from the way we've been brought up; the way we've been taught to understand who we are."

This, of course, can be challenging to hear. I don't press it. We all—whether kids or adults—need to understand how this kind of self-reflection, self-awareness, can improve overall performance and enhance well-being. "This ability to look at yourself from inside is the first step in becoming really good at something," I tell the kids. "Self-awareness is the ability we have to observe and evaluate our own experience. When you observe yourself, you can make adjustments. The trick is to learn to observe your experience without getting down on yourself. One way to do this is to remember that we are always observing to *learn*. When we remember that it's all about a love of learning, self-observation becomes much easier to do. Sometimes, it's still hard. But it can also be exciting and fun."

Not everyone gets it all the time. But as a teacher, when I see children (or adults, for that matter) start to understand and implement these ideas, it's powerful. Knowledge is a gift that we fully embrace when we share it with others, knowing that they will do the same. It is a beautiful, empowering, and humbling process.

FOR SOME YOUNGSTERS, HOWEVER, THE TEACHINGS DON'T LAND. Mostly, they're really good kids, and they want to do what I ask them to do. But in certain cases the students don't own it. They're just going through the motions because they think they should. They're following expectations imposed on them from the outside.

Under their willingness is an insecurity that can be heartbreaking. They're simply doing what other people want

them to do. They're being who they think they *should* be, not
who they really *are*.

Part of the problem is that educators (and our society) have a
"one size fits all" expectation of kids. We want them to grow
up and be "productive members of society." We gauge their
potential using certain prefabricated measures. But we do kids
a grave disservice when we don't acknowledge that there are
multiple ways we learn and many different types of intelligence
that need to be nurtured. Some of us have a spatial intelligence;
some of us are strong in the area of language; some of us have
emotional intelligence, which has to do with understanding
the complexities and nuances of relationships; still others
have what I would call existential intelligence—they seem
to intuitively know how to navigate the human fear of death
and retain a balance and poise in the face of feeling alone and
powerless.

When I teach kids, I always tell them how quiet and shy I was
when younger, how I slid into a painful and difficult descent
into addiction, and how my redemptive journey of recovery
began with giving myself over to my love of learning and became
about teaching in order to learn and to keep what I've learned in
recovery by giving it away.

Kids often come up to me after I speak and confess to me how
hard it is for them to function sometimes. They're often shaking
and crying as they tell me this. I believe they allow themselves to
be open with me because I am very vulnerable when I speak—
and this is especially true when I speak to kids. I don't come at

them like some big bad-ass authority figure. Being with kids, I express the shy, vulnerable child who still lives inside me.

I will sometimes talk to kids in middle and high school about my relationship with numbers. "I don't know why," I say, "but numbers always spoke to me. Can you believe that I did income tax returns for all the members of my family from the eighth grade on? When I looked at numbers, the relationships between them were clear. They made an instant, intuitive sense. It was the same thing when I worked in cost accounting—I could hear the numbers talking.

"We generally live in a universe where one plus one equals two. But there is another universe. I know some of you are going to think I'm crazy when I say this, but there's a universe in which one plus one does *not* equal two. I'm not talking literally, of course. We all know that in order to get by in this world, we have to be able to make one plus one equal two. We've got to be about what works and is practical. We have to make a living, and we need to take care of that and keep our eye on the ball and be able to perform. Still, there's something more. I know that you want me to tell you what it is, and yet it's impossible to put into words. We can talk around it and over it and under it and even right through it, but we can't quite hit it.

"We may not be able to say exactly what it is, but we can feel it. And I know that *you* know that your heart doesn't know anything about arithmetic. Your soul isn't controlled by algorithms, although I'm sure those marketers in Silicon Valley wish that it were. And you know what? Sometimes life doesn't just add up.

"Is it weird that some dude who is good with numbers with a good job and a good salary just gave it up, walked away and did something else, which led him to be standing up here and talking to you today? Maybe so. It takes trust. It takes being able to make mistakes and not get down on yourself. It takes being able to realize you have a choice, even when you think you don't. If you remember one thing about our talk today, let it be this—you *always* have a choice."

For those kids who are into math and science, I'm careful to make sure that they feel supported in what inspires them. I tell kids that everyone is different, and they may find their greatness within through numbers. I certainly think that's true for gifted mathematicians and physicists. And music has a math to it as well. Numbers represent harmony—they have given us so much that is beautiful and useful. I make sure that kids know that what I'm saying is they didn't fulfill *me*. For a guy who did cost accounting and financial analysis for his professional life, it was no easy thing to admit that my real interest was elsewhere. But it's often the case that we need to let it all go—security, money, who we think we are—in order to walk the path of seeking, of finding out who we *really* are and what our lives are truly about.

In the classroom, however, I restrain myself. I know that many kids hear from their parents that they should do well in school (learn all about the ways in which one plus one equals two) to prepare them to go out and get a good job. I don't want to push them too hard in another direction, toward the unknown and unquantifiable. The last thing many parents want to hear is that their kid, after listening to George Mumford and becoming

"Mumfied," as Phil Jackson used to put it, has decided to go wander through India and become enlightened. And that's not what I want either. What I do want is for them to feel less impaired by their mistakes, to instead see mistakes as challenges and as a path to growth. I want them to understand that it is only through the struggle that we gain the mental toughness and fortitude to succeed. That it is only through trying and failing that we build inner strength. And that at their young age they should begin to consider this as a *lifelong* process; they can (and even should) begin looking at life this way starting *now*.

It's particularly poignant to see kids falter and stumble and not know how to pick themselves up. You can actually see them crumple and shrink inside. And yet the same painful mechanisms of self-criticism and self-doubt are at work when we're adults.

Perhaps the key lesson I try to instill in kids is that our mistakes are about learning and growth rather than inadequacy and failure. Next time you find yourself getting down on yourself about something you've done, something that feels mistaken or misguided or has led to what you perceive as unfortunate consequences, ask yourself: What do I need to learn here? How can this experience help me grow? I mean really *look*. Don't just give it superficial lip service. Ask with absolute sincerity and real curiosity. Be a witness to your own internal processes. If you consistently and sincerely do this, I bet you will find that you will be less driven by your initial reactions and become self-aware. Observe yourself from inside yourself with a spirit of curiosity. This is a technique that I stress not only with kids but also with professional athletes and corporate CEOs. It is a key to freeing the mind, body, and spirit.

INDELIBLE INTERCONNECTIONS

The men's swim coach at the US Naval Academy in Annapolis had given his team my book *The Mindful Athlete: Secrets to Pure Performance* for summer reading. The response was positive. When school resumed, he reached out to me to see if I was interested in coming to the Academy to work with the team. This was a rare chance to reach a group of people who might otherwise never brush up against mindfulness and meditation. These were future leaders in the Pentagon and in politics and public policy—a very different group than those I usually coached.

These young men were being trained to be soldiers, to be warriors. I was eager to talk to them and help develop their humanity as well. I wanted to expose them to what it means to be a spiritual warrior.

The most important aspect of spiritual warfare is being able to lead with the heart. This holds true even in the inhumanity of war. I wanted them to develop an awareness of the divinity inside themselves, which we all share. I am not a pacifist. I believe that sometimes you have to match the intensity of what's coming at you. You have to meet the challenge, whatever that may be. But we should always have the awareness first and foremost that the person we are acting against is a child of God. The spiritual

warrior recognizes the divinity inside even people whom we feel
the impulse to demonize.

In his remarkable poem "Please Call Me by My True Names,"
inspired by helping Vietnamese boat people during the Vietnam
War, Zen master Thich Nhat Hanh writes:

> *I am the twelve-year-old girl,*
> *refugee on a small boat,*
> *who throws herself into the ocean*
> *after being raped by a sea pirate.*
> *And I am the pirate,*
> *my heart not yet capable*
> *of seeing and loving.*

In this excerpt, Thay—the author's affectionate nickname, which
means "teacher" in Vietnamese—is pointing to the illusion of
separateness. He is the girl *and* the pirate, as we all are, no matter
how difficult that may be to grasp. When we do violence to each
other, we are most often disavowing our innate connectedness.
To acknowledge this is to awaken to the compassion that exists
inside us. As the poem puts it, "evil" (in the form of the pirate
in all of us) is not yet capable of seeing our true nature, which
abides in love.

At times we feel how connected we are to each other. We felt
it in the wake of 9/11 and the Boston Marathon bombing and
the wildfires in California, for example. We also felt it in the
pandemic, as we watched incredibly brave health-care workers
put their lives on the line to help others. I have nieces who are

nurses, and they were out there, doing what needed to be done, even as our hospitals were overflowing. And I have a cousin who is a health-care worker who came out of retirement to help when the waves of sickness struck. How can we not be in awe of their selflessness, dedication, and commitment? That kind of attitude of service translates into all areas of life in all our interactions with people. When we're a positive, willing, loving presence, we are helping create a world in which we all want to live. Heaven is not some distant realm where we go after we die. It's inside all of us, and we can manifest it in our interactions with each other in the here and now.

What is in us that gives us that capacity? Where does the impulse for altruistic selflessness come from? Why does the firefighter run into a building that's on the verge of collapse? Why will some people run toward the flames rather than away from them? Hemingway famously said that courage is "grace under pressure." That's a beautiful definition. We might go further and also acknowledge that one set of preconditions that allow this grace to manifest can come from the desire to be of service.

Many of the cadets at Annapolis were there because they wanted to serve their country. They hoped heroism would find them. Some of them, at least, were ready to lay down their lives in the line of duty.

I was especially aware of this noble calling at the formal dinner the Academy threw in my honor. Everyone was wearing their dress whites, and there was snap and vigor in the pristine uniforms. In fact, there was a palpable pageantry about the whole

place, a formality that wasn't stiff at all, as I had anticipated;
it was energizing, as though a tingling voltage was setting
everything humming. The cadets themselves weren't at all what
I had expected. I hadn't anticipated the depth of their questions
or what I felt was their openness to meditation and mindfulness
practices. And I was surprised when they looked to me for
wisdom. "What happens when your commanding officer gives
you an order you don't believe in or is against your values?" one
cadet asked.

I felt a familiarity with the formality of the atmosphere of
Annapolis. It was rather like some of the Buddhist monasteries I
had visited and spent time in. There was the same adherence to
schedule, a dress code, numerous daily rituals, clearly enforced
hierarchies, and communal meals. The Academy and monasteries
both molded people in a tradition they were consciously
adopting. In both cases, there was a kind of surrender, a giving
over of one's self, and an acceptance of austerities. At the same
time, I was also surprised by the similarities of the cadets to
student athletes in traditional college settings. The cadets went
home for the summer just like regular students. The conference
room and the swimming pool area where I worked with them
were the same as at any other college. At times it was easy to
forget that I was in a military setting.

When I was at the Academy, my mind kept returning to my dear
friend Joseph, a helicopter pilot who had served in the Vietnam
War. He then became a conscientious objector, left the military,
and went to Thailand, where he took his vows and became a
Buddhist monk. He lived a monk's life for twenty years. He

eventually disrobed and returned home to the United States, and we hired him to teach in prisons with me.

Joseph was a perfect fit to work with the inmates because he'd spent many years operating in some form or fashion in an environment similar to theirs: first in the army's Seventh Cavalry as a captain and helicopter pilot and then in Buddhist monasteries. Prison was just another variation on that theme. A prison, like the army or a monastery, had strict hierarchies, regimens, uniforms, and the same sense of an inner world with its own codes that one needed to follow and which was set apart from the outer world, which came to be viewed by those on the inside as a place of lawless, reckless freedom. Joseph was a tremendous ally and teacher. He was able to connect these two disparate worlds, which helped me and the many prisoners he taught better understand the complexities of the universe. Those in the military are not just automatons hell-bent on violence as the solution, nor are those monks living in isolation trying to escape reality for their own selfish reasons. The reality is far more nuanced and inspiring. Part of unlocking is accepting people where they are and for who they are. Teaching mindfulness in a military setting may seem like a contradiction in terms, but it's not. It's important not to distance ourselves from areas of life that may not conform to our inclinations and values. We need to constantly be reaching, creating bridges between us and people who make different kinds of choices than the choices we might make. This is the essence of growth, and it's a lifelong process.

I have felt compelled to work with law enforcement, the military, corrections officers, and public safety officials. In all cases, I see my job as helping them unlock and access the divinity inside themselves. It's my hope that the mental tools of following the breath, inner observation, finding one's inner strength, and accessing the masterpiece within will bring calm and compassion to the many trying situations they often face. Corrections officers and prison staff, for example, often need to deescalate situations, and those mental tools help them do that. Prison can be a pressure cooker; inmates not infrequently come to a boil. On one occasion, I saw a corrections officer calm an agitated inmate using the breathing techniques I had taught him. He had the inmate breathe through his anger and upset. But more than that, I saw the CO calm *himself* before he approached the inmate. He accessed the eye of the hurricane. Being calm himself, the CO created an atmosphere of trust and compassion, which transformed the way he did his job and helped make the prison a more humane place. When we are peaceful inside, we bring peace to those around us.

LOCUS OF CONTROL

Let's come back to kids for a moment.

I've recently been working on a "Mindful Athlete" online course for high school and college kids. The idea for the course came out of a series of presentations I gave at the Confluencenter for Creative Inquiry, an interdisciplinary research institute at the University of Arizona. One of those presentations I gave over a two-day period was at a high school that was renowned for having a challenging student body. There had been talk of shutting the school down. I was warned to expect the worst, yet my experience was the opposite.

The students were attentive, engaged and engaging, and not in the least disruptive or oppositional. They welcomed me with open arms.

After the presentation, I said to members of my team: "We need to do more to connect with everyone struggling in our world today. The world is upside down for these kids. Of course, that's true not just for kids but for many people. Still, I think it's particularly important to help our children. What can we do to help them feel less anxious and hopeless?" Thus was born the idea for the online course.

When I work in schools, it's very clear to me that much of the fear and despair our kids are feeling is a result of the ubiquitous presence of social media. When you're holding your phone in front of your face for hours each day and getting constant feedback on all your posts and having to compare yourself to celebrities and influencers and measure your number of "followers" against everybody else's, and all this is happening twenty-four/seven, it's no wonder that people generally, and particularly impressionable young people, feel tentative and shaky.

The digital world is always echoing inside us, and it can be hard to distinguish what's happening on the screen from the real world for kids. Let me rephrase that—digital reality *is* their real world. Where, I ask you, is the "locus of control," a term we use in psychology when discussing agency to distinguish the internal from the external? If the locus of control is *external*, it means that society or perhaps our ideas of status or the opinions of other people—something outside us—is dictating our behavior. When our locus of control is *internal*, it means that our decision-making process is in accord with who we are inside, not with the messages coming at us. What's particularly difficult about today's ubiquitous handheld devices is that they become appendages. It's hard to know where the hand stops and the phone begins. In a sense, the phone becomes part of the person. Through this technology, the external is internalized in new and vexing ways. Thus kids have what psychologist and author R. D. Lang would call a "divided mind," which is a real problem. The Bible is wise on this point. It says that the "double-minded man is unstable in all his ways" (James 1:8).

Add to this problem the way COVID-19 has affected social life and the overall sense of safety. As if that weren't enough, students' feelings of safety and security have also been impacted by the never-ending rash of racist attacks and school shootings, and the escalating crisis brought on by climate change. The nastiness of the political atmosphere and culture gripping our country isn't doing anything to help young people's state of mind either. No wonder they—and we—struggle.

I wrote my master's thesis in psychology on teenage suicide. I learned that the major factor determining whether or not teens at risk die by suicide is whether or not they feel that there's someone in their life who loves them unconditionally. This is vitally important for all of us. When we can begin to experience the greatness within, we feel loved. Unconditionally. We discover a greater capacity inside ourselves, something bigger and more powerful. We know our perfection in all its imperfect humanness. And we want to help other people feel that way too.

RECENTLY I'VE BEEN WORKING WITH APPROXIMATELY SIXTY HIGH schools and fifty or so middle schools in Suffolk County, New York. Initially, the interest came from the district's athletic programs, but then it generalized: the schools saw that what I was teaching could help the general student population.

One of the aspects they particularly appreciate about my teaching, I've been told, is that I don't give the kids any answers; what I want them to do is find things out for themselves. The children need to *experience* mindfulness, right effort, trust, insight, and confidence. Without personal experience of these things, they're just a bunch of words.

As I've noted above, we always want a formula to help us grow, to free us from pain, to help us gain confidence, to make us wiser and better human beings. But there *is* no formula. That's why I find it essential to draw wisdom and insight from all traditions. The question is always: Why am I reacting the way I am reacting? What is driving that? How can I see clearly in this moment? How can I generate hope? How can I keep my connection with the divinity inside me? And, finally and most important, how can I serve? How can I help?

What does it mean, I often ask the kids I teach, to keep generating hope? How can we embrace whatever comes up and say yes to it? "The most fortunate people in the world," I say, "are not the people who are rich or famous but those who are able to live in a state of energizing *enthusiasm*."

They get it. Even steeped in our relentlessly materialistic culture, they know there is something else, something beyond and greater than. They know that their online "metaverse" is sapping their soul.

ENERGIZING ENTHUSIASM

How can we keep being enthusiastic? It's a perplexing question, especially in today's world, where there are so many overwhelming problems. It's all too easy to despair.

Where does enthusiasm come from anyway? Is it something that "possesses" us? Or is it perhaps part of our temperament, with some of us just naturally more enthusiastic than others? Does enthusiasm have to do with our genes, or is it the result of the way we were raised? All these factors count, but I know from my own experience that we can also *generate* enthusiasm. My enthusiasm is sustained by my hunger to learn, which is only increasing as I get older. As long as I have that, I am being drawn into the future. There is a feeling of excitement in the process of becoming. What is going to happen next? Each moment is pregnant with possibility.

We make much of being "in the now" when we talk and write about mindfulness. Wisdom teacher Eckhart Tolle writes about honoring the now as "the only time there is. . . . Make sure the present moment is your friend, not your enemy. Honor it by giving it your fullest attention. Appreciate it by being thankful for it. Become internally aligned with it by allowing it to be as it is." Doing all these things will inevitably also generate enthusiasm.

We can all practice being in the now. How do we focus our attention on the present moment? If we feel distracted or scattered, we can always come back to the breath, breathing in and out slowly, following the breath moving out of our body, coming back into our body. How do we feel thankful for the present moment? By realizing that we are alive, that we have breath in our body. We align with the present moment by allowing it to be as it is, by coming into the breath and into the body and out of the ego-inflected mind, which wants to control everything and thinks it knows best and is constantly trying to assert itself.

Honoring and appreciating and being thankful for the now are important steps, both for themselves and as ways to boost enthusiasm. Another indispensable part of generating enthusiasm has to do with our hope for the future. A lack of enthusiasm signals a kind of pessimism about or indifference to not only what befalls us personally but also what happens to those we love, the whole skein of our relationships, and the fate of our world. Enthusiasm looks forward. It is a moving thing, not static or stationary, and it has to do with a continuum of feeling as though we're developing and growing. Too often we think we have been somehow "completed" at some point in the past. That we have already done all (or most) of our growing and learning. Unlocking means committing to continuing that process, to actually accelerating it through our lives. I can honestly say that I am more enthusiastic now than at any point in my life. And my enthusiasm just keeps growing.

We can think of enthusiasm as having two components: learning and accomplishment. Learning involves being able to see things in new ways, not simply accumulating information. Learning is about the moment when we say: I never thought of it that way before—I didn't see that connection or relationship between things. When we learn something, we *change*; we become what we're learning rather than just gathering information about it. We can read about fishing, or we can have an experience of fishing. To learn to fish, we must fish. To know about fishing or think about fishing is not fishing. As the proverb goes: To know and not to act is not to know.

Achievement, the second component of enthusiasm, is not about winning a game or having people tell us we're great. Accomplishment has nothing to do with kudos or recognition in the eyes of the world. It is a feeling inside us.

The word *enthusiasm* comes from the Greek *entheos*, meaning "the God within." When we connect with our authentic self—the self that feels connected with the ten thousand things—we feel the God within. We feel the unfolding of life moment by moment, along with a sense of awe, as we do when we're in a flow state. Something is carrying us. We're connected to a truth that is greater than our ego, the small self that is always insisting on "Me! Me! Me!" and saying, "I'm gonna get mine!"

With true enthusiasm, there is no calculation, no playing the angles, no staging, positioning, or posturing, no calculation of pluses and minuses. It is the math of one plus one equals six! There is a spontaneous unfolding that we're part of, though it's hard to grasp because it is both a "now" and a "then." That unfolding has been named a silence, an emptiness, but in my experience it can also have a propulsive quality, a sense of movement. For me it is often *active*, kinesthetic.

I have often worked at the intersection between stillness and movement. My preferred kind of mindfulness is active. It is not about sitting on a cushion contemplating emptiness. It is mindfulness on the go, being in flow and in the moment, yet in motion; it is when we're at our most active, most dynamic. When movement comes out of the stillness, there's a knowing, a wisdom of what to do, how to do, and when to do. The seeing and doing co-arise without a hair's breadth between them. In fact, it's more about being than doing because there is no doer. Something larger than ourselves is speaking and acting through us. And we know: this is what we were born for—it is the be-all and end-all, the alpha and the omega.

Think about the enthusiasm unleashed by children. It is contagious, it is active, and it is sacred. It is about abiding in love. About the spontaneous joy of being in love with life. It is available to all of us to tap into. Thich Nhat Hanh writes about it in "Please Call Me by My True Names," the poem quoted earlier:

> *I still arrive, in order to laugh and to cry,*
> *to fear and to hope.*
> *The rhythm of my heart is the birth and death*
> *of all that is alive.*

UNLOCKED

————

Free your mind and your ass will follow.

—Funkadelic

The people who formed Alcoholics Anonymous in 1935 wanted to ensure that the program they came up with, which was contingent on a belief in a higher power, would work for people from all religious denominations and would not be offensive to atheists and agnostics. In referring to that higher power, they also used the term "a power greater than ourselves," which really could be anything, although AA also stipulates that it should be loving and caring. All of us need to establish a relationship with a higher power if we want to unlock.

Some of us may feel squeamish around such language. We may think recognizing a higher power means that we're going to walk around with stars in our eyes and a false sense of benevolent intelligence looking out for us when clearly no such thing exists.

Friendly or unfriendly? Isn't that an anthropomorphic way of looking at this unimaginably vast and infinitely unknowable universe?

That's the point. The question has to do not so much with cosmic nature but with our temperament. How do we generate hope? How do we live with an energizing enthusiasm? It's difficult to do if we feel we live in an essentially hostile environment. In fact, that's an awful way to live. It clouds our mind and separates us from the joy of being alive, and, most important, from loving each other. We feel as if it's us against them, or us against a hostile universe. It often can feel as though the cards are stacked against us.

Shit happens. But so do beauty and joy. That's why it's crucial that we're able to deal with difficulties and disappointments in a way that brings us back to what matters: a feeling of gratitude for this life we've been given. Otherwise, what's the point? We don't want our energy sapped, leaving us feeling cold and removed. We want to be warm and connected. How can we do that? By making conscious connection with a higher power. I love Einstein's claim, quoted in an earlier chapter, that our most important decision is whether we perceive the universe as friendly or hostile, but I think Funkadelic said it best: "Free your mind and your ass will follow."

A HIGHER POWER REALLY COULD BE ANYTHING "GREATER THAN ourselves." My partner has a nephew who's an Orthodox Jewish man, and he and his wife are raising their children in the rigorously observant Orthodox manner. I have had a close relationship with one of their boys. From a young age, he has been curious about me. He and the male members of his family and community dress in *tzitzit* (fringes) that dangle from a special four-cornered garment called a *tallit*. I obviously dress very differently. My skin color is different too. One day when he was about eight years old he asked me: "George, what's your concept of God?" I was tickled by the precocious question, and I was also moved. Here was this little kid who was being raised as an Orthodox Jew and had a very clear idea of God even at his young age; but he was genuinely interested in how someone else might think about what for him was an all-important "higher power."

I pondered for a moment and then pointed to an electrical outlet in the wall. "I think about God like plugging into that socket," I said.

I could see the light turn on in his eyes. "Yeah," he said. "Like a power or a force."

"Exactly."

A perfect example of a higher power at work. We could think of it as that which connects us to each other. Which enables us to give each other hope and lift each other up.

KNOCK AND IT SHALL BE OPENED

My concept of a higher power has changed over the years. Until I was fourteen years old, I went to a Southern Baptist church every Sunday with my friends and cousins. I dressed up in my meeting clothes—a white shirt and tie or maybe a clip-on, and whatever suit I had. The church was an imposing building which, in memory, is near what was then Dudley Street Station in Roxbury (as in Dudley Do-Right). The congregation was 100 percent African American—not one white person to be found in the pews. The preachers were all male, and there was an organ that was liberally used during the service. Other than that, I don't remember much; my boys and I went through the motions, though we all felt we'd rather be somewhere else. Still, we went. Every Sunday.

My mother sent us, although she never attended herself. "They sin for six days and then on the seventh they think they can get away scot-free," she said. "They try to get redemption and forgiveness and then they backslide and do all the same old things that they know are wrong." She was a tough-minded lady.

Still, she wanted us to have church exposure as children. Her father had been a preacher.

I had my own Bible, and it was special to me in some way that is hard to define. I kept it close, but I didn't talk about it to anyone. I kept my money hidden in its pages. I took it with me to college, although again I kept it hidden from others. Not that I was ashamed of it exactly, or of my churchgoing boyhood. It just felt as though it was something private, for me alone.

After church, my pals and I might go to the movies downtown, or over to a friend's aunt's house for Sunday dinner. Always fried

chicken, potato salad, collard greens, and cornbread. We ate like
ravenous wolves. The chicken was crispy outside and steaming
inside, and we picked the bones clean. As delicious as it was,
though, chicken wasn't what we were there for. The true stars
of those meals were the desserts: sugary cakes with voluptuous
swirls of icing. I didn't get enough to eat at home. I was always
hungry, and those cakes were heaven on earth.

After I turned fourteen, we moved out of Roxbury into
Dorchester, from a mostly Black neighborhood into a
neighborhood that was mixed, perhaps even predominantly
white. In Dorchester I went to church only on Easter and for
weddings and funerals. And it wasn't just because of the move.
In my teenage mind, church was trying to tell me what I could or
could not do. It was trying to *force* me to behave in a certain way.
I already had the streak inside me of not wanting anyone to force
me to do what I didn't want to do. If you tried that, you had
better watch out, because you'd have a tiger by the tail.

My relationship with God was remote. I didn't have a lot of faith.
Yet somehow through all of it I did become familiar with the
Bible—its language, stories, and wisdom—and that stuck with
me; in fact, it has been an anchor in my life. Christian scripture
came to me by way of implicit or nondeclarative learning. It is a
blur to me, probably because I wasn't fully there. I was already
lost in my inward fantasies, the hideouts that had taken a strong
hold of me even at a young age.

My relationship to the Bible often surprises people. Never more
so than when I was invited to present to about one thousand

employees of Lululemon Athletica, a Vancouver-based apparel
company. They were holding an employee retreat at Whistler
ski resort in British Columbia. The vast majority of attendees
were female and young. They were stylish and hip and enmeshed
in twenty-first-century spiritual pursuits such as yoga and
meditation. I was one of three speakers and gave a twenty-
minute talk and then took questions. One young woman asked
me: "What book would you recommend we read?" Before I
even had time to think about it, "The Bible!" popped out, and
people laughed because it was so clearly inadvertent. "That
answer kind of surprises me," I added. "I've been reading a book
a week for many, many years. But recommending the Bible
makes sense. Every hotel has the Bible in every room, so you're
covered. You don't have to pack a book for your trip and carry
that weight."

I think they understood that I was joking, although not
about recommending the Bible as an indispensable text.
Throughout the years, Bible-based lessons have spontaneously
come to me without any prompting, blending in with the
Buddhist teachings I've studied and practiced: the lessons
of mindfulness and compassion. They also colored the
various schools of psychology that absorbed me as a graduate
student, and in which I continue to immerse myself, and they
informed the science of mind-body that also became part
of my repertoire. When I'd speak, before I knew what I was
saying, aphorisms from the gospels would rise to my lips. One
that I often recited was: "Ask and it shall be given to you;
seek and you shall find; knock and it shall be opened to you"
(Matthew 7:7).

What will be given? What will we find? What will be opened?

The response to these questions is what we have been talking about all along: the greatness within, the masterpiece inside us that is our authentic self, our original face.

"Knock and it shall be opened."

In other words, unlock.

A DOUBLE-MINDED MAN

My connection with a higher power is one of the things that have made it possible for me to maintain my sobriety. Getting high just isn't an option now. I'm not sure why that's the case for me but not for so many others. Why was I able to get clean and sober and stay that way while so many people that I knew were active alcoholics and drug addicts even after starting recovery? Part of the reason is because I really came to see that God isn't out there somewhere. Divinity is within. That's where we will find it. It's not in some other place and some other time. It's a presence that is here now.

When I got clean and I began working with drug addicts in the programs that I managed, one of the things I quickly realized is that addicts have the gift of gab—and a complete lack of integrity. By that I do not mean that they were in any way bad people. When I note their lack of integrity—and mine too, incidentally, while I was using—what I'm pointing to is that

what they *said* about what they were going to do and what their
plans and intentions were was completely different from what
they actually ended up doing. They spun a web of fantasies
around what they thought that their therapist or counselor
wanted to hear. And they had the patter down pat: they could be
maddeningly persuasive.

Another lesson from the gospels rang true for me: "Be careful
to do everything they tell you. But do not do what they do,
for they do not practice what they preach" (Matthew 23:3).
This is the addict's MO, saying one thing and doing another.
The true person is hidden under the skein of words the addict
weaves. That is both infuriating and heartbreaking for people
who care about the addict. You can count on addicts to do only
one thing—whatever it takes for them to keep feeding their
addiction.

My work with addicts taught me the value of integrity and
honesty. Watching addicts in their hideouts made me more
acutely aware of my own system of hideouts. It was fortunate for
me that when I came out of detox, I had what might be called a
powerful born-again experience: the whole world was numinous,
made afresh, and there was an immanence, or the feeling of spirit
descending. As I mentioned earlier, I knew that the person who
had walked into detox wasn't the same person who walked out
of it. I was ready to leave my hideouts, to come clean, to stop
living a double life. *A double-minded man is unstable in all his
ways.* That instability makes recovery impossible. Relapsing is
almost inevitable, and I was determined not to go that route. I'm
writing here about detox and addiction and recovery, but please

remember that hiding out and being double-minded are not confined to drug addicts and alcoholics—we all do those things.

At the point early on in my recovery when I was doing mind-body work, I started to examine the different parts of who we are and how those different parts of us fit together. Often called the sleeping prophet, clairvoyant Edgar Cayce, in a quote I love, said: "For the spirit is life; the mind is the builder; the physical is the result." There it is again: Get your mind right and your ass will follow.

Without connection to spirit, what will the mind build? What will we see as the physical result? These are questions worth thinking about, especially as they apply to our world today.

How do we get beyond our perceived separateness? How do we awaken our compassionate hearts? How do we make peace with the greed, jealousy, and hatred inside us? The answer is found in the deep insight of Thay's poem "Please Call Me by My True Names," portions of which I shared in the previous chapter. That insight, the *illusion* of separateness, is a radical teaching. It calls us to identify with the sea pirate, to see that on a fundamental level there is no separation between us and the sea pirate. We are also, of course, individuals. It's another paradox we have to live with, always mindful of the insight that a rigid absoluteness of *no* separation—the narrow view—runs counter to the Buddha's approach that we should take the Middle Way: not too much of either this or that. When we take the Middle Way we are in a position to embrace the full complexity of who we are. This does not, however, give us license to collapse into moral relativism or a wishy-washy spinelessness that refuses to take a stand. From that Middle Way, we must accept and act on the illusion of separateness. Until we stop separating ourselves from each other needlessly, claiming the moral high ground and punishing each other for transgressions, we will *all* continue to suffer, and we will be doomed to repeat the same cycle of violence and hatred that has plagued us from, well, the beginning.

To be capable of true transformation we must feel loved. I do recognize how difficult, almost impossible, it is to feel love from or show love to people who are being cruel, selfish, or hateful. Still, the fact remains that if we want things to change and the world to become more compassionate and loving, that is really the only option.

SOME WEAK-ASS SHIT

In the work of the great Sufi poets Hafiz and Rumi, the higher power is sometimes referred to as "the beloved." But we humans aren't always open to that higher power. Rumi writes: "Your task is not to seek for love, but merely to seek and find all the barriers within yourself you have built against it." This love he's speaking of is generalized, not focused on the idealization of one person and thus by nature transient. It is an ambient feeling that informs our lives.

It is not easy to live in this openness to love. As I read the religious existentialists—writers such as Søren Kierkegaard and Martin Buber—early on in my recovery, I was deeply impressed by their fearlessness. They clearly faced and accepted that we are born alone and we die alone. I realized as I read them that I had felt lonely much of the time throughout my life. They helped me understand why I felt the way I did; and in the process, I began to be honest about what I came to see as the root of my addiction. It stemmed from a feeling of loneliness, of isolation and separateness, that caused an ache inside, a need for something to assuage my feelings of aloneness. I wanted connection, to feel as though I belonged to and was part of something larger than myself. I got that feeling when I was in flow on the basketball court. It's not coincidental that when that was no longer available to me, because of the injury to my ankle in college, my addiction bloomed.

Kierkegaard points at selfless love, the love that destroys the separateness of the ego, as an antidote to the loneliness of our existence. He writes in *Fear and Trembling*: "No! No one who was great in the world will be forgotten, but everyone was great in his own way, and everyone in proportion to the greatness of that which he loved. He who loved himself became great by virtue of himself, and he who loved other men became great by his devotedness, but he who loved God became the greatest of all. . . . Abraham was the greatest of all, great by that power whose strength is powerlessness, great by that wisdom which is foolishness, great by that hope whose form is madness, great by the love that is hatred to oneself."

The selfless love that Christ or the Buddha or Abraham embodied—the practice of which requires a "leap of faith" as Kierkegaard calls it—shatters our rational, rule-bound mind.

Embodying paradox and mystery, it may seem to be foolishness, even madness. This and only this will get at the "root" of the problem. The rest is prevarication—or, as Funkadelic might say, some weak-ass shit.

DIVINE SPARKS

At their heart, all paths to wisdom are the same path. The religious existentialists taught that the search for self-knowledge is about peeling back the layers of the onion until you get to the core, the nub. That is the Buddha's teaching too: a stripping away of our conditioning to arrive at the core of who we are. One of the things that people discover when they develop self-awareness is that there's a hidden self that they're not really copping to. Both Buddhists and the existentialists say that in that emptiness exists our freedom, our responsibility to choose.

In *The Way of Man*, the great Jewish existential philosopher Martin Buber writes about our hiddenness—and our potential: "Everyone has in him something precious that is in no one else, but this . . . something in a man is revealed to him only if he truly perceives his strongest feeling, his central wish that is in him, which stirs his being. . . . The world is an irradiation of God but as it is endowed with an independence and striving, it is apt, always and everywhere, to form a crust around itself. Thus, a divine spark lives in every thing and being, but each such spark is enclosed by an isolating shell."

We've talked about the greatness within and the masterpiece within. The way Buber talks about the divinity that resides in each of us has been crucial to the way I've thought about how we can fulfill our potential. Buber wisely notes that the masterpiece is revealed when we perceive our truest and strongest feeling. This is our own true self vibrating inside us, singing to us, stirring our soul. This is the divine spark that exists inside each of us.

Unlocking is about freeing the divine spark from the encrusted shell around it. That shell could be thought of as our hiddenness or our conditioning. As Buber describes it, that enclosing shell is built up naturally, perhaps even inevitably. It is part of what it means to be human—an independent, striving being. We are embodied creatures; and just as the divine spark exists inside each of us, so too it is concealed. The unlocking process could be thought of as a cracking of the shell to let that spark go free, much the way in the blaze of a fire sparks fly up into the night. Buber might say those sparks are returning to their source— another way of thinking about a higher power.

PERSONAL RESPONSIBILITY

My first Buddhist teacher, Larry Rosenberg, whom I've talked about in earlier chapters, was instrumental in my early recovery. In AA meetings you begin by saying, "Hi, my name is George, and I'm an alcoholic." Or "Hi, my name is George, and I'm a drug addict." Larry saw that I was becoming attached to that definition of myself; it was another way for the ego to create a little domain where it was in charge. We all do that—I am a such-and-such or a so-and-so. It gives us a kind of security, an identity that we parade around in the world. We become attached to this definition of ourselves. We cling to it and hide in it, and it subverts the spontaneous expression of our authentic self: who we really are.

Larry saw that defining myself as an addict was limiting me. A kind of self-fulfilling and self-perpetuating prophecy, the label "addict" worked like a set of handcuffs that would keep me from real growth. He encouraged me instead to talk about being in recovery, which is the language that I still use today to describe my journey away from drugs and alcohol and my enduring commitment to sobriety.

I discovered early on to base my recovery on learning and growth. That was part of why I did the introductory class most weeks at the CIMC for six years: I wanted to drill its content into my bones. I took the same approach to reading. I committed to reading at least a book a week, as I mentioned earlier—a vow I've kept. I also made a promise to myself that I would read any difficult passage in a book over and over until I understood it. It didn't matter if I had to read it one hundred times. In the past, if I hadn't understood something, I'd quickly skipped over it and moved on.

When I was working with the Lakers and the Bulls, I would go to AA meetings occasionally and also to Al-Anon meetings, which are for the families and friends of alcoholics; but the meetings weren't a constant in my life in the same way that prayer, meditation, reading, and service were—and are. The meetings weren't something I felt bound to in order to keep myself clean and sober, although for some people they're lifesaving. When I go to meetings, it's because I want to go, not because I have to go. As I said, I've never been very good at having other people tell me what to do, and I've never been keen on following someone else's program about what's supposed to be good for me. I've charted my own way and made my own choices and created my own path in life after digesting various wisdom traditions that have appealed to me.

Although I'm persistent, that doesn't mean I'm unteachable or uncoachable. Way back when I was first getting into AA, one of the things I had to learn was how to listen and interpret. For example, to really absorb the eleventh step of the Twelve Step program—the step that deals with turning your will over to the higher power or the will of God—I had to translate "higher power" into my own terms. Some people look at the eleventh step as a surrender, a giving up of autonomy and our free will, foundations of our independence and self-sufficiency. That perspective can be useful for some people. But it didn't feel right for me. I came to see the giving over of oneself in another way—as a kind of generosity. It's not really a sacrifice or renunciation or letting go. But it took some time and struggle for me to get there.

IN THOSE EARLY DAYS, I COULDN'T SIMPLY GET MY MIND RIGHT for my ass to follow—in other words, I couldn't think my way into proper behavior. Eventually, yes—but before I could do that,

I had to reverse-engineer: I had to *behave* my way into proper thinking. So whatever they told me to do, I had to do—"They" being those grizzled old-timers, the chain-smoking guys who ran the meetings back in the 1980s. Those dudes, who had seen it all, with their endless cups of coffee and their raspy laughs and their tattooed forearms, were rough, man. They told me in no uncertain terms that I had to take the cotton out of my ears and sit up in the front of the room and "act like you don't know anything." And they were right—that's exactly what I needed to do. They had various sayings, some of which have stuck with me: for example, "I can't, He can, so let Him." My attitude, taken from those meetings in smoky rooms, has been: Do what you need to do, and the next step will be given to you. This applies not only to Twelve Step meeting rooms but to all of life—to the locker room, the boardroom, the classroom, and the meditation hall.

As I've noted before, a big part of any self-discovery journey is taking personal responsibility, which requires courage. This is true of recovery in the most general sense—that is, recovery not just from addiction, but also from past trauma. Recovery of any kind is really about taking responsibility for ourselves. We have to get past what I call B&D, blame and denial. Our human tendency is to want to blame others for what befalls us, for all our injuries and frustrations, denying our own part in why we feel the way we do. This is one way we hide out. We all know, at some level, that our lives are in our own hands. We know that it's our responsibility to manage our responses—no one else's. If we feel bad, that's on us. Yet we always have myriad reasons why it's someone else's fault (blame). Or why we're incapacitated or unable (denial).

If we are (or were) sexually or physically abused, we may find it difficult to accept that we can't (or couldn't) control the circumstances of the harm done to us. But we can control our response to it, both in the moment and looking back. When we simply *react*, we become victims; instead, we need to *respond*— that is, draw on our divine essence, our inner worth and strength, and consciously *choose* what we will do or say. We don't get to judge either—not ourselves and not our perpetrator. We can't take refuge in moral rectitude, which is often one of our hideouts. We have to accept that the abuse happened, and we have to relate to it in a way that ensures we don't lose ourselves or our humanity—and also ensures we keep our connection to our power source. By these means we are able to break the illusion of separateness with its corollary of self-centered fear.

I needed to come to this sort of acceptance in my own process of recovery, having grown up with an alcoholic father in a household where if you didn't shut up you got beat up. Part of my addiction came from the feeling of being victimized, and it deepened when I got hurt and couldn't play basketball anymore. In recovery, by connecting with a higher power, I embraced a process that changed my consciousness.

One way my mind got right was that I realized some of my strengths were actually weaknesses and some of my weaknesses, strengths. Part of the "ism" in my alcoholism was thinking I could control other people's behavior through my actions. In other words, if I shut up and disappeared into my own little world, my father would stop drinking. I was trying to be perfect, and I thought that if I became perfect, the fucked-up-ness all around me would evaporate. I had to realize that instead of trying to fix people, I had to let them fix themselves. I was loyal to a fault, loyal to people whom I shouldn't have been loyal to. And most of the time I was compliant—too compliant. It was part of my loving, empathetic nature, but there was no way I knew how to express that love in a way that served me or anyone else.

My weaknesses were pretty much like just about everyone else's: fear, insecurity, and doubt. In my recovery I turned them into strengths. I investigated them, and in doing so I came to understand myself better. What is fear? What is anxiety? Where do these feelings come from? What am I feeling insecure about? If we ponder these questions and really dig into them, we often realize what my buddy the late philosopher Alan Watts used to say: "There is wisdom in insecurity." Human beings are always seeking security. We fear impermanence, and yet there is no permanence. Everything changes. Looked at in this way, we begin to see that fear and insecurity are the roots of wisdom.

Doubt is different than fear. Doubt indicates a lack of understanding. When we're curious about something and we want to understand it—that is, when we feel doubt—that's a different psychology than when we're afraid of something and running away from it. Doubt is acknowledging that we don't understand how the universe works. But doubt always comes back to aligning with divinity or aligning with how things are. There's an inherent lawfulness about our world, even when we're confronted with apparent evidence to the contrary. This is a friendly universe. We might wish for things to be other than they are; we all do that. But

I'll say it again—we all have greatness inside us. We need to take personal responsibility for our lives, for who we are. This is not something that is in any way limiting, however. After all, it's not the size of the dog. It's the size of the bite.

"RECOVERING" OUR TRUE SELVES

If we're not honest with ourselves, we are "double-minded," as we've seen. There is a gap between what we really want and feel, why we act the way we do, and how we perceive ourselves. We are unstable, which is another way of saying we lack confidence. Confidence comes from being honest with ourselves, being able to admit to ourselves where we hide out.

It's incumbent on each person to ask: Where are my hideouts and when do I use them? How can I come clean, not just if we're addicts? The process of recovery applies to all of us, addict or not. We all want to be able to "recover" our true self, the masterpiece within. We want to crack our encrusted shell and access the divine spark inside us, to release that spark and share it with the world. Like the caterpillar in the chrysalis, we need to be able to embrace the struggle. No struggle, no swag. The recovery of our authentic self is the same process, whether we're in the gym, in the meditation hall, or at work.

RECOVERY FOR ME IS ABOUT SHOWING UP—AND CONTINUING TO show up. It's about remembering to remember that in order to find myself, I have to lose myself; it is about coming back to the fundamental truth that teaching is the best way to learn. I often ask people (whether or not they're addicts): What does your recovery look like? How can you feel more fully yourself? How can you strip away habitual behaviors that don't serve you?

To learn and to serve—these things give our life meaning and purpose. The pure performance that I practice and preach has to do with continuous growth, with entering the flow of life. It is about coming back into the present moment while keeping our eye on our goals. We joyfully embrace the paradoxes of effortless effort and movement out from the eye of the hurricane.

We have the capacity to generate hope and enthusiasm and to keep opening ourselves to the full range of experience. It is helpful, in this regard, to remember that the Buddha taught the Middle Way, a path that embraces moderation in all things. The Middle Way keeps us from dogmatic extremes and rigidity. It helps us stay in flow. We are able to thread the needle of paradox and opposition. We can be in the present and still look to the future. We can feel the oneness of all things and still keep our eyes on the prize. Life can move in us and through us and we can still feel a very real sense of personal accomplishment. We can lose ourselves in effortless effort and the goalless goal and still be passionate about winning. Profound feelings of existential aloneness and powerlessness are counterbalanced by being able to pick ourselves up and focus on our divine essence, which connects us to all things.

We are all, in one way or another, on a hero's journey. The particulars of that journey are different for each one of us.

Yet there are profound similarities in what we all experience. Strength and beauty and love reside inside each of us. Our masterpiece is not symbolic; it is very real. When we get in touch with it, we unlock vast resources and find we have the capacity and desire to not only help ourselves but be of service. To give to others. We overflow. We find there are no boundaries between us and the world. In this way, we experience the illusion of separateness. We forget ourselves and find ourselves.

You are already on this journey, and I hope this book will serve as a steadfast companion. May it be a source of encouragement and help. May it open your heart, energize your being, and guide your steps. May it awaken gratitude inside you for your life.

That is what my own journey has given me. I am more grateful now than at any point in my past, even on that amazing day when I walked out of rehab and realized I was free from my imprisoning addictions. That same sense of wonder and newness now infuses my daily life. What's more, I now know that nothing can disturb my peace. I don't let anything come at me unless I call it. I take my cue from Jesse Ventura in *Predator*. When the little dude told Ventura he was bleeding, Ventura responded, "I ain't got time to bleed."

What I do have time for is the feeling of being in flow, the experience of life unfolding around me and in me. I continue to wake up every day with the desire to learn and grow and serve. We all have that potential, but it has to be developed. It's an inside job. With it, all things are possible. When you're in flow, there's only one way to go. Onward and upward.

To keep it, you've got to give it away. To learn it, you have to teach it. And to teach it, you have to be it. Likewise, to know and not to act is not to know. You've got to *be the message*. My own life is a reflection of this ability to fully unlock. And I hope that you—through the experience of reading this book—also feel that potential.

Being unlocked is not about *doing* but about *being*. Doing comes out of being. If you want an excellent life, you have to be excellent. The idea is not to go to heaven; it's to grow to heaven. If you want love, you have to be love. When you change the way you look at things, the things you look at change.

The message is really very, very simple. I invite you to take it in. Feel into it. We all have the ability to recover our authentic self, to find the greatness within and unlock. We can find flow, access the divine spark. Again, it's an inside job. We all want to bring what is uniquely ours into the world. We are all part of a larger becoming and unfolding. We are all connected. We're in it together.

Learn and serve. Serve and learn. Recover your true self, the masterpiece within, and bring it forth, out into the world. Share it. That is how I live, and I invite you to live that way too.

EPILOGUE

When I heard about Kobe's death, I was at the University of Richmond, watching their Division I women's basketball team. I was sitting courtside when my phone went off, a notification from one of those gossip-mongering sites announcing that Kobe had been killed in a helicopter crash. That is one sick joke, I thought to myself, and I went back to following the game. But then my sisters started calling, asking if I was okay. They didn't know where I was, but they knew that if I was out in LA, I might be with Kobe; and, sisters being sisters, they wanted to make sure I was okay. They also knew the loss would be painful for me, as it was; in fact, it continues to reverberate to this day. I often think of a conversation I had with him when he was about to retire from basketball.

"People sometimes say I'm 'locked in,' but that's not it," he said, referring to the times when he'd been in flow or in the zone and had performed at a particularly high level. "When you're there, it's something that's free and easy. It's not about being 'locked.' It's about being *loose*."

"That's right," I said. "It's really about *unlocking*. It should feel perfectly natural and unencumbered. It's about just being. Just doing. The way a river flows."

"Or the mamba moves!"

How I miss that cat. There will never be another like him.

The rabbis say that when a person dies, a whole world dies with them. What a world Kobe built in his short, intense life.

Kobe's death is a great example of the Buddha's fundamental teaching of impermanence—that everything changes, that nothing is here to stay. Kobe's death has added urgency to my desire to help people unlock and access the divinity inside them. Until we do that, it's impossible to recognize it in others. And this is why it's so important that we find it in ourselves.

That is my definition of success.

ACKNOWLEDGMENTS

I would like to thank the people below, as well as those whose names I've probably, unpardonably forgotten, for their wisdom, friendship, and support.

My family: Edye N. Merzer, my love and life partner; and Emma Mumford (deceased) and William Mumford (deceased), my mother and father.

Siblings: William Mumford Jr. (deceased), Pearl Hughes (deceased) and Martin Hughes (deceased), John Mumford (deceased), Betty Jenkins, Barbara Tucker, Edith Hicks, Juanita Mumford, Evelina Mumford (deceased), Linda Wilson (deceased) and Harry Wilson (deceased), Donald Mumford and Dawn Kelley, Mary Trotman, and Gregory Mumford and Dr. Piper Smith-Mumford.

Relatives: Mary Taylor, my maternal grandmother; Aunt Sister (deceased) and Uncle Joe Smoot (deceased); Rick Lanier (deceased); Darren Kelley; Darryl Hilliard; nieces and nephews (including great and great-great); cousins and relations; and Carol Merzer (deceased).

Coaches and staff: Phil Jackson, Tex Winter, Jim Cleamons, Stephen Kerr, Al Skinner, Andrea Leonard, Dr. Tom Mitchell, and Dr. Kevin Pallis.

EOTH staff: Steve Hailey, Greg Berg, Lia Aliberti, Rocco Aliberti, and Ryan Berg.

Friends: Julius Erving, Michael Jordan, Scottie Pippen, Kobe Bryant, Shaquille O'Neal, Jack Kornfield, Trudy Goodman, Sharon Salzberg, Joseph Goldstein, Larry Rosenberg, Narayan Liebson, Jon Kabat-Zinn, Tara Brach, Dan Harris, Michael Murphy, Jill Wesley, Joan Borysenko, Robin Casarjian, Roland Lazenby, John Reed, Eddie Carle (deceased), Mark Campbell, Fred Zackon, Lucie McInnes, Fatima Mbodj, Jimmy Lawson, Nikki Geannelis, Joseph Kappel, Bill Kennedy, Troy Bell, Craig Smith, Sean Marshall, Reggie Jackson, Laura Georges, Kia McNeill, Nancy Legan, Maddy Klyne, Diana Kamila, Jewell Lloyd, Divock Origi, Jessica Pegula, Charlie Smith, and Julius Thomas.

Prison teachers and staff: the Mindfulness-Based Stress Reduction program (Center for Mindfulness at UMass Memorial Medical Center, Worcester, Massachusetts).

The clients and organizations who have participated in the unlocking are too numerous to mention by name.

My publisher, HarperCollins, and staff: Gideon Weil and Maya Alpert.

Peter McGuigan, my literary agent and friend.

Aardvark and staff.

Special thanks to Kenneth Wapner, my collaborator; Ken has been an indispensable part of the process of bringing this book to life. He was there with me every step of the way. I couldn't have done it without him, and I am tremendously grateful.

ABOUT THE AUTHOR

George Mumford is a psychologist, elite performance expert, and author with an unforgettable personal story. He was an aspiring basketball player at the University of Massachusetts when injuries forced him out of the game he loved. The medications that relieved the pain of his injuries also numbed him to the emptiness he felt without the game and eventually led him to heroin.

After years of practicing meditation and getting clean, Mumford enrolled in Dr. Jon Kabat-Zinn's Mindfulness-Based Stress Reduction program and collaborated with him to create the Inner-city Stress Reduction Clinic in the early nineties.

When Michael Jordan left the Chicago Bulls to play baseball in 1993, the team was in crisis. Coach Phil Jackson, a longtime mindfulness practitioner, contacted Dr. Kabat-Zinn to find someone who could teach mindfulness techniques to the struggling team—someone who would have credibility and could speak the language of his players. Kabat-Zinn led Jackson to Mumford, and their partnership began.

Mumford has worked with Jackson and many of the teams he coached to become NBA champions. His roster of champion clients has since blossomed way beyond basketball to include corporate executives, Olympians, and athletes in many different sports.